Life Woven into God

Life Woven into God

Sermons for the Lectionary, Year B,
Pentecost through Christ the King

BRUCE L. TAYLOR

WIPF & STOCK · Eugene, Oregon

LIFE WOVEN INTO GOD
Sermons for the Lectionary, Year B, Pentecost through Christ the King

Copyright © 2020 Bruce L. Taylor. All rights reserved. Except for brief quotations in critical publications or reviews, no part of this book may be reproduced in any manner without prior written permission from the publisher. Write: Permissions, Wipf and Stock Publishers, 199 W. 8th Ave., Suite 3, Eugene, OR 97401.

Wipf & Stock
An Imprint of Wipf and Stock Publishers
199 W. 8th Ave., Suite 3
Eugene, OR 97401

www.wipfandstock.com

Unless otherwise noted, Scripture quotations are from the Common Bible: New Revised Standard Version Bible, copyright © 1989 National Council of the Churches of Christ in the United States of America. Used by permission. All rights reserved worldwide. Emphasis added.

Scripture quotations marked (RSV) are from Revised Standard Version of the Bible, copyright © 1946, 1952, and 1971 National Council of the Churches of Christ in the United States of America. Used by permission. All rights reserved.

Scripture quotations marked (GNT) are from the Good News Translation in Today's English Version, Second Edition, copyright © 1993 by American Bible Society. Used by Permission.

PAPERBACK ISBN: 978-1-7252-7646-8
HARDCOVER ISBN: 978-1-7252-7645-1
EBOOK ISBN: 978-1-7252-7647-5

Manufactured in the U.S.A.   10/23/20

In memory of Sister Rose Denise, SL,
and Sister Charles Regina, SC.
Requiescant in pace et gaudio.

Contents

Introduction   xi

Day of Pentecost   1
Ezekiel 37:1–14, Acts 2:1–21, John 15:26–27; 16:4b–15
"Where the Spirit Is"

Trinity Sunday   6
Isaiah 6:1–8, Romans 8:12–17, John 3:1–17
"Nicodemus' Diary"

Ninth Sunday in Ordinary Time   13
1 Samuel 3:1–10, 2 Corinthians 4:5–12, Mark 2:23—3:6
"God Has No Law against Love"

Tenth Sunday in Ordinary Time   18
1 Samuel 8:4–20; 11:14–15, 2 Corinthians 4:13—5:1, Mark 3:20–35 (GNT)
"And They Said, 'He's Gone Mad!'"

Eleventh Sunday in Ordinary Time   23
1 Samuel 15:34—16:13, 2 Corinthians 5:6–10, 14–17, Mark 4:26–34
"To See Aright"

Twelfth Sunday in Ordinary Time   28
1 Samuel 17:1a, 4–11, 19–23, 32–49, 2 Corinthians 6:1–13, Mark 4:35–41
"God on Board"

Thirteenth Sunday in Ordinary Time   33
2 Samuel 1:1, 17–27, 2 Corinthians 8:7–15, Mark 5:21–43
"The Priorities of God"

Fourteenth Sunday in Ordinary Time   38
2 Samuel 5:1–5, 9–10, 2 Corinthians 12:2–10, Mark 6:1–13
"Strength through Weakness"

Fifteenth Sunday in Ordinary Time — 43
2 Samuel 6:1–5, 12b–19, Ephesians 1:3–14, Mark 6:14–29
"Predestined for Glory"

Sixteenth Sunday in Ordinary Time — 48
2 Samuel 7:1–14a, Ephesians 2:11–22, Mark 6:30–34, 53–56
"And the Walls Came Tumbling Down"

Seventeenth Sunday in Ordinary Time — 53
2 Samuel 11:1–15, Ephesians 3:14–21, John 6:1–21
"Fish, Loaves, and Faith"

Eighteenth Sunday in Ordinary Time — 58
2 Samuel 11:26—12:13a, Ephesians 4:1–16, John 6:24–35
"Growing Up Together"

Nineteenth Sunday in Ordinary Time — 63
2 Samuel 18:5–9, 15, 31–33, Ephesians 4:25—5:2, John 6:35, 41–51
"Rogues to Riches"

Twentieth Sunday in Ordinary Time — 67
1 Kings 2:10–12; 3:3–14, Ephesians 5:15–20, Mark 6:51–58
"A King's Wisdom"

Twenty-first Sunday in Ordinary Time — 72
1 Kings 8:1, 6, 10–11, 22–30, 41–43, Ephesians 6:10–20, John 6:56–69
"Where We Meet the Infinite"

Twenty-Second Sunday in Ordinary Time — 77
Song of Solomon 2:8–13, James 1:17–27, Mark 7:1–8, 14–15, 21–23
"When Cleanliness Is Next to Godlessness"

Twenty-Third Sunday in Ordinary Time — 82
Proverbs 22:1–2, 8–9, 22–23, James 2:1–17, Mark 7:24–37
"It All Begins Here"

Twenty-Fourth Sunday in Ordinary Time — 88
Proverbs 1:20–33, James 3:1–12, Mark 8:27–38
"Words on Words"

Twenty-Fifth Sunday in Ordinary Time — 93
Proverbs 31:10–31, James 3:13—4:3, 7–8a, Mark 9:30–37
"The Greatest"

Twenty-Sixth Sunday in Ordinary Time   101
Esther 7:1–6, 9–10; 9:20–22, James 5:13–20, Mark 9:38–50
"Life Woven into God"

Twenty-Seventh Sunday in Ordinary Time   106
Job 1:1; 2:1–10, Hebrews 1:1–4; 2:5–12, Mark 10:2–16
"Are You Too Grown Up for the Kingdom?"

Twenty-Eighth Sunday in Ordinary Time   111
Job 23:1–9, 16–17, Hebrews 4:12–16, Mark 10:17–31
"Stripped-Down Faith"

Twenty-Ninth Sunday in Ordinary Time   117
Job 38:1–7, Hebrews 5:1–10, Mark 10:35–45
"Faith"

Thirtieth Sunday in Ordinary Time   123
Job 42:1–6, 10–17, Hebrews 7:23–28, Mark 10:46–52
"Lessons Over a Stale Biscuit"

All Saints' Day   130
Isaiah 25:6–9, Revelation 21:1–6a, John 11:32–44
"Anticipation"

Thirty-first Sunday in Ordinary Time   134
Ruth 1:1–18, Hebrews 9:11–14, Mark 12:28–34
"Love Beyond the Law"

Thirty-Second Sunday in Ordinary Time   139
Ruth 3:1–5; 4:13–17, Hebrews 9:24–28, Mark 12:38–44
"Sacrificing"

Thirty-Third Sunday in Ordinary Time   144
1 Samuel 1:4–20, Hebrews 10:11–25, Mark 12:41—13:8
"What Impresses You?"

Evening before the National Day of Thanksgiving   149
Joel 2:21–17, 1 Timothy 2:1–7, Matthew 6:25–33
"The Most Difficult Commandment"

Christ the King   154
2 Samuel 23:1–7, Revelation 1:4b–8, John 18:33–37
"Where Jesus Reigns"

Appendix: "Living Water" 159

List of Sources Cited 167

Introduction

I DON'T RECALL THAT my preaching professor ever stated a goal for our class other than that we learn to "preach effectively." Each student probably had a more existential target in mind, ranging from simply surviving in the pulpit to ending up in a particular size of church or meeting denominational requirements for ordination. We might also have shared some more aspirational hopes along the lines of changing the lives of parishioners, our communities, maybe even our world with the words we spoke during the eighteen minutes each Sunday morning allotted to communicate the gospel.

According to my concordance, the word "preach" occurs only ten times in the New Revised Standard Version of the Bible, and seven of those appear in the *Hebrew* scriptures, not in the New Testament. The word "preacher" occurs only once, in Micah, and there are three instances of "preaching," one each in Acts, Galatians, and 1 Timothy. None of the usages is definitional, but all presume that the hearer or listener already knows what the words "preach," "preacher," and "preaching" mean. The word "sermon" appears not at all. But this does not mean that the modern preacher has a clean slate upon which to invent the meaning of these terms.

Contrast this paucity with the abundance of references to the word "prophet" and its related forms. Although there are no definitions of that word in the Bible either, to my knowledge, the plethora of instances of what the Old Testament prophets said and did, and later appeals to the prophets' words and deeds in the writings of the New Testament, offer enough examples that we can construct a general picture of their role. Of course, there are warnings against *false* prophets, and the problematic news that the truth or falsehood of the person claiming to be a prophet will not be known until the credibility of that person's witness is proven or disproven by later events. But scripture discloses that the true prophet is someone who speaks on behalf of God, having been called and commissioned to do so through a process more or less unique to each individual and not always witnessed or accepted by other people.

While "preacher" is not a term unknown in Old Testament times, the concept of "prophet" seems to have been much more familiar. The inclusion of "prophets" among the spiritual gifts listed in Ephesians 4:11 and "prophecy" at 1 Corinthians 12:10, and the absence in these verses of the words "preachers" and "preaching," suggests the early church's understanding that the function of the preacher in New Testament times was to speak on behalf of God, communicating the divine perspective with regard to matters of life and faith, in a manner somewhat different from that of two other spiritually gifted Christian leaders, specified in Ephesians as "pastors" and "teachers."

Of course, we do not know the exact leadership functions in every early congregation and should not impose our own notions of ecclesiastical organization on the ancient church. The situation of modern credentialed preachers is not exactly equivalent to that of the prophets of old. In the tradition of mainline connectional denominations, admission to the pulpit requires a series of human acknowledgments of fitness and competence that, while designed to detect God's calling and commission, are not quite the same thing. And whereas the scriptural prophets seem to have been called and commissioned for specific prophetical assignments, ordination usually constitutes a lifelong license to preach.

But there is no distinction in the *substance* of what ancient prophets and modern preachers were and are to communicate. At least in the Reformed tradition, people are entitled and should expect to hear from the lips of the preacher, as hearers heard from the truthful prophets of old, a message from God about how to respond to contemporary situations and events as those who are in covenant with God to be faithful and obedient hearers and doers of the Word. And that places an obligation upon the preacher to be prayerful, studious, honest, and bold, even while remaining faithful and sensitive to her or his pastoral obligations as well. The primary difference between the Hebrew prophets, as depicted in the scriptures, and preachers, in the daily experience of the church of Jesus Christ, is that the latter are expected to function within the full constellation of what it means to be a minister of Word and sacrament. Whereas that will include what is commonly phrased as "speaking truth to power," from which no one who understands and accepts the prophetic side of Christian ministry should shy away, "preacher" will always be but one (albeit major) dimension of the more encompassing description of summoning and helping people to weave their lives into the ongoing purpose of God.

In my preaching ministry, I have attempted to help people discover and participate in God's purpose in every aspect of their lives, taking such practical forms as participating responsibly in the public forum and knowledgeably selecting products from the grocery shelf and faithfully fulfilling the joyful and sober duties of congregational membership. Caring for the poor and the sick and the stranger and the outcast should command the attention of the humblest Christian and any government which he or she can influence. Viewing every situation from the perspective of the health and dignity of God's tiniest creature and whole societies and ecosystems is the calling and commission of every believer. Placing hope in the God who brought each of us into being and loves each of us for eternity and offered the costliest of sacrifices to cement our relationship with our divine parent is the sustaining motivation and the comfort and privilege of everyone whose heart is open to the gospel. The preacher cannot force those results, but everything that the modern-day prophet, the contemporary spokesperson for God, does, not *only* in the pulpit but *especially* in the pulpit, should provide a picture of what a life woven into God will be like.

Here, in this collection of sermons for the latter half of the Christian year featuring the Mark cycle of the Common Lectionary (Revised), in sermons for Sundays and for feast days, I hope that the reader, whether in the academy or the parish or at home, will find testimony to the task of the congregation-based prophet and the task of those who would hear and respond to the preacher's words as being the Word of God communicated through sermon, and as an invitation to weave oneself into the garment of eternal life that God desires to bestow upon each of us.

Day of Pentecost

Spanish Springs Presbyterian Church, Sparks, Nevada
June 4, 2006

Ezekiel 37:1–14
Acts 2:1–21
John 15:26–27; 16:4b–15

"Where the Spirit Is"

ONE CAN HARDLY IMAGINE a more depressing and discouraging scene. An entire valley littered with dry, bleached bones, the painful reminder of the destruction of a nation and the waste of the nation's youth. Ezekiel, one of the exiles taken away to Babylon when that nation's army defeated Judah by battle and by siege, found himself looking out upon a vast field of hopelessness. Death was all around him. There was not a chance that any of the soldiers was still alive, for their flesh had all decayed or been picked away long since. And he heard a voice asking him, "Mortal, can these bones live?" (Ezek 37:3a NRSV). Silly question, it would have seemed to most people. Cruel, even. Sons, brothers, fathers cut down in the prime of life in a worthless cause. The end result was the same as if these soldiers had never *taken* to the battlefield. Israel was no more. Judah was no more. Jerusalem was no more. Even the temple was no more. And for all the good he had done them, it was just the same as if *God* were no more. But Ezekiel, in what might have been one final murmur of piety (or was it perhaps a daring expression of bitter resentment?), responded only, "O Lord GOD, you know" (37:3b NRSV). It is possible that Ezekiel thought that God was rubbing his nose in the ignominious slaughter, and so he was throwing it back at God in the sarcastic way that we might say, "Well, what do *you* think?"

There was an ancient Israelite notion that the created world and everything in it is kept alive by the ever-renewed pouring out of the breath of life from God. It's almost as if the Spirit of God were an invisible fluid permeating and pulsing through the whole world and giving it life as God directs. Death and corruption seize upon the world, or upon a person or a community, whenever God withholds his Spirit. To Ezekiel's mind, then, considering the utter devastation as far as his eye could see, God must certainly have withdrawn his Spirit, breath, wind, not only from these soldiers, now just anonymous skeletons, but from the entire nation that had always thought it was God's special people. And even though the disaster had been their own fault, the penalty for their faithless idolatry and their faithless disregard of God's commands, the people were dismayed to realize that their nation had fallen, and that that meant God had withdrawn his vital and sustaining presence from them. "Mortal, can these bones live?" "O Lord God, you know" (37:3 NRSV).

"Then the Lord God said to [Ezekiel], 'Prophesy to these bones, and say to them: O dry bones, hear the word of the Lord. Thus says the Lord God to these bones: I will cause breath to enter you, and you shall live. I will lay sinews on you, and will cause flesh to come upon you, and cover you with skin, and put breath in you, and you shall live; and you shall know that I am the Lord" (37:4–6 NRSV). So Ezekiel prophesied as he had been commanded, and as he prophesied,

> suddenly there was a noise, a rattling, and the bones came together, bone to its bone. [Ezekiel] looked, and there were sinews on them, and flesh had come upon them, and skin had covered them; but there was no breath in them. Then [God] said to [Ezekiel], "Prophesy to the breath, prophesy, mortal, and say to the breath: Thus says the Lord God: Come from the four winds, O breath, and breathe upon these slain, that they may live." (37:7a–9 NRSV)

Ezekiel prophesied as God commanded him, "and the breath came into them, and they lived, and stood on their feet, a vast multitude" (37:10 NRSV).

So it must have been when the followers of Jesus felt dejected and bewildered when he told them to wait for something they did not understand and he was taken up from them into heaven. They had certainly felt devastated when he was put to death, but then he had appeared to them three days later, in his crucified body, complete with the wounds made by the nails and the sword, but alive again, and he taught them and encouraged them and even ate with them for forty blissful days, and then he disappeared and it was as if the very breath of life had been given back and then taken away again. But, to their credit, they stayed together, hopeful, trustful, faithful. And when the day of Pentecost came, the Jewish holiday that was seven

Sundays after Passover, "they were all together in one place. And suddenly from heaven there came a sound like the rush of a violent wind, and it filled the entire house where they were sitting" (Acts 2:1b–2 NRSV). And all of the disciples, mainly Galileans, commonly thought to be unsophisticated and certainly *not* schooled in foreign languages, began to *speak* in *other* tongues, so that they could be understood by the foreign peoples who had made pilgrimage to Jerusalem for the festival. The people around them were amazed and astonished and perplexed, though some "sneered and said, 'They are filled with new wine'" (2:13 NRSV).

But Peter—the same Peter who had been so pitifully timid on the night Jesus was arrested—stood up and said that they weren't drunk. It was a matter of the prophecy of Joel being fulfilled—God was pouring out his Spirit. And then the disciple-become-apostle went on to preach about the crucifixion and resurrection of Jesus of Nazareth. Peter had never done such a thing in all the episodes recounted in the Gospels. He had never spoken so eloquently; he had never understood so clearly; he had never declaimed so boldly. What had made the difference in Peter? What made the difference in *all* of the followers of Christ spoken of in the book of Acts? As far as Luke is concerned, it was the presence among them of the Holy Spirit.

Whatever the *details* of the bestowal of the Spirit upon the followers of Jesus, clearly the *effect* was to inspire them to do great and wondrous things that they had never done before, had never been *able* to do before, had never even *considered* doing before. As the coming of the Spirit upon Mary brought life to a virgin womb, so the coming of the Spirit upon the followers of Jesus brought life to a group of people otherwise fearful and cowardly. And as the coming of the Spirit to a young peasant woman in an unremarkable desert village brought together all of history in a focus of divine purpose, so the coming of the Spirit upon Christ's disciples brought a unity of motive and commitment that set in motion the greatest human adventure in all of history—the miraculous spread of the church. "In the last days it will be, God declares, that I will pour out my Spirit upon all flesh, and your sons and your daughters shall prophesy, and your young men shall see visions, and your old men shall dream dreams," Joel had promised (2:17 NRSV). And not only prophesy and see visions and dream dreams, as it turned out, but proclaim and write words of life, work miracles of healing and restoring, and dare to do what every *reasonable* person knew to be *impossible*.

As a fish does not know what water is, as a bird does not know what air is, those of us who have been in the church most of our lives may take for granted the extraordinarily wondrous atmosphere in which we live and move and have our being—this Spirit of God that flows through the new creation that sprang into existence on that first *Christian* Pentecost. It was not only *Peter* who was given new life and finally was able to stand on his feet, stand up to critics, stand up for what he had come to know was the truth. Multiply Peter by scores, and hundreds, and thousands, and millions, working for cures in the face of skepticism, sharing generously in the face of greed, witnessing boldly in the face of persecution, testifying bravely to the Lord of life in the face of cross and fire and sword. Consider the joyful sacrifice of time, treasure, ability, recognizing that all these things belong to God and we have them only as a trust, in lessons of faith taught, in fortunes given away, in doctors healing the indigent. Remember a Polish bishop embarrassing a tyrant out of office, an African bishop embarrassing a racist society into becoming a true democracy, a Salvadoran bishop whose stubborn refusal to be silent about the carnage of his people led to his *own* assassination, which, in turn, finally focused the world's attention on a campaign of genocide funded by a nation that proudly calls itself free and democratic. Think of a frail woman walking the dirty streets of an overcrowded city looking for the sick, whom society considered expendable, of a white man and a black man from the segregated American South working side by side to end the cruel exploitation of native rubber plantation workers in the Congo, of a teenage girl testifying to her faith at the deadly end of an assault rifle in the library of a suburban high school. Recall a young theologian feeling compelled finally to participate in a plot to bring an end to one of history's cruelest dictators, of the Stated Clerk of our own denomination being arrested for marching against racial segregation, of a young executive quitting his job rather than be party to an act of corporate fraud. "All were amazed and perplexed, saying to one another, 'What does this mean?' But others sneered and said, 'They are filled with new wine'" (2:12–13 NRSV). "'They don't know what they're talking about.' 'They're going to wreck the economy.' 'They should stay out of politics.' 'They should mind their own business.' 'They're not being realistic.'" "In the last days it will be, God declares, that I will pour out my Spirit upon all flesh, and your sons and your daughters shall prophesy, and your young men shall see visions, and your old men shall dream dreams" (2:17 NRSV).

Like many people who have read that passage about the one unforgiveable sin—blaspheming the Holy Spirit—I have pondered just exactly what "blaspheming the Holy Spirit" means. I've come to the conclusion, based on who the Holy Spirit is, and considering what the Holy Spirit has done, that blaspheming the Holy Spirit means saying that something that *God wills* to happen is impossible, whether it be the redemption of any situation, the forgiveness of any sinner, the salvation of any individual. For *that* would be to say that the Holy Spirit is impotent, that the Holy Spirit is unavailing, that the Holy Spirit is a lie. But your and my very being here together, sinners forgiven and forgiving each other, remembering together the teachings and commands of Jesus Christ, our very love for God and for each other, ought to be impossible, so contradictory as it all is to the values and habits of the world. "Mortal, can these bones live?" (Ezek 37:3a NRSV). "O Lord God, you know" (37:3b NRSV). "Prophesy to these bones, and say to them: O dry bones, hear the word of the Lord. Thus says the Lord God to these bones: I will cause breath to enter you, and you shall live. I will lay sinews on you, and will cause flesh to come upon you, and cover you with skin, and put breath in you, and you shall live; and you shall know that I am the Lord" (37:4–6 NRSV).

Where the *Spirit* is, there is truth being proclaimed. Where the *Spirit* is, there is justice being done. Where the *Spirit* is, there is unity that transcends differences. Where the *Spirit* is, there are wounds being healed. Where the *Spirit* is, there are hungry people being fed. Where the *Spirit* is, there are lonely people being visited. Where the *Spirit* is, there are strangers being welcomed. Where the *Spirit* is, there are outcasts being included. Where the *Spirit* is, there are eyes and ears and hands and hearts being opened. Where the *Spirit* is, there is life being breathed into what was as good as dead. Where the *Spirit* is, bread and wine are being broken and poured and the Lord's death is being proclaimed until he returns. Where the *Spirit* is, *there* is the true church of Jesus Christ.

Trinity Sunday

Spanish Springs Presbyterian Church, Sparks, Nevada
June 7, 2009

Isaiah 6:1–8
Romans 8:12–17
John 3:1–17

"Nicodemus' Diary"

ATTENDED A MEETING OF the elders today. Much was simply trivial routine, as the Roman procurator does not permit us to deal with anything that he deems to be political or would infringe on his administration of Roman law and justice. We did have appear before us a rabbi from Jericho, whose teachings on some points of the Torah seemed to require correction. On the whole, he submitted unquestioningly to our authority in matters of interpretation of the law, though some of the elders warned him that they would be alert to any deviations from the tradition. And there was also some talk about a Nazarene—a rabbi, some of us suppose, although that is rather unclear, especially since the rumors are that he has violated the sabbath on multiple occasions, which scarcely seems possible for a rabbi. So the council of elders spends its time these days—hardly the way things were in Moses' day when the seventy were appointed to help him govern the people. Not that anyone wants to return to the wilderness, but God's presence with the people seemed more direct in those days.

Attended another meeting of the council of elders. No new information about the situation in Jericho—the rabbi whom we dealt with last time—but more about this Nazarene fellow. Talk of a miracle he performed at a wedding in Cana. Rather sketchy and unreliable, in my opinion. Who can trust reports from a drunken wedding party? A few of my colleagues very agitated at the news of water being turned into wine. At most weddings I've attended, it goes the other way—the longer the party goes on, the more like *water* the *wine* becomes. The wise host knows that some people will *eventually* drink *anything*.

Emergency meeting of the council today, called to address the matter of this rabbi or teacher or whatever from Nazareth. The news is, he came to Jerusalem yesterday and immediately caused a scene at the temple, turning out the money changers and letting the sheep and cattle out of their pens—the ones that are on hand to be purchased for making sacrifices. The money changers and vendors are rapscallions, of course—and resented by the common people, deservedly so, profiting as they do on the good intentions of the pious. But it was apparently a most unseemly performance by the man, who came to town with a number of his followers and now has won to himself several others. Of course, preparations for Passover are consuming the time of most of us, and the coming to Jerusalem of the Passover crowds is what makes that man's behavior such a sensitive issue just now. I have no idea why the temple guards didn't step in. It seems that the man just walked out of the temple after having his say and having his way with the profiteers. One of the elders wanted to charge him with desecrating the temple, although, of course, cleansing the temple of the money changers was hardly a desecration—in fact, in my book, just the opposite! Good riddance!—though, of course, it would make it inconvenient to pay the temple tax. Furthermore, he seems to have upset some people who confronted him about his authority for doing such things—he answered them by saying something about destroying the temple and raising it back up in three days. I rather distrust the accuracy of that report. Who could say something so absurd? I pointed this out in the council. Others said that it wasn't right for anyone to be so disorderly and disruptive in the temple. No matter what we might think of the money changers and sellers of the sacrificial animals, they were there legally and performing a necessary function and ought to be able to do so without some crazy Galilean coming in and causing them trouble. Seems to me that there might be more behind this man's behavior than insanity, though. Some of our number volunteered to try to be present at some of the man's gatherings to collect evidence about just what it is he is saying and doing, whether he is twisting the scriptures that he quotes. I personally have more important things to be doing as the Passover approaches.

Another emergency meeting of the council of elders today. There are reports that the Nazarene is performing feats of magic around town as well as teaching about the scriptures in a new way. People are saying that he preaches with confidence and certainly speaks words that ring true. Not sure that what he is doing should be called "magic"—doesn't sound like he's just doing things to *impress* people, but to *help* them, including several reports of healing and exorcism and the like, especially among the lower classes. Poor souls, can't afford doctors, quite likely. They're probably delighted to have someone pay them some attention and take their complaints seriously enough to try to do something about them. Still, he's dabbling where someone who's not a *physician*—or a *priest*—shouldn't. I'm starting to sense trouble ahead.

One of my colleagues today persuaded me to go with him to hear the Nazarene. His name is Jesus, and he seems to have come to the city from Capernaum. Of course, there are a lot of Galileans and all sorts of other people coming to town for the Passover. I must say, I was very impressed with him, though it was a little disconcerting that he did not invoke the authority of the *rabbis* for what he had to say. No, he just taught as if on his *own* authority. What he said certainly moved many of the people who were listening—plain language, speaking straight to the heart, as it were, telling people to repent of their sins but also that God is merciful. Then, when a man in the crowd shouted out asking for healing for his deformed foot, Jesus went to him and told him to take a few steps. The man objected that it was too difficult, but Jesus told him to do it anyway, and the man did so, and said that he had been healed. I couldn't get very close, but the people around the man were turning to the crowd and shouting that the man's foot had been straightened! And then Jesus put his hand on some people's heads and blessed them, and then he left, followed by some of the crowd as others dispersed to go on their way. I admit, there is a personal magnetism about him. But if he's going about performing healings without the approval of some higher authority, well, that's irregular. Still, the man can walk upright now, without limping.

I went out to hear Jesus again today, this time on my own. The same sort of thing happened as yesterday—teaching the same sorts of things that the prophets wrote, but somehow fresh and pertinent for our own day, and some more healings of people with various ailments. But there was something more—he forgave a woman who confessed to being a sinner. Now, that seemed to be going too far. Only *God* can do that. The woman whom he forgave—who knows what sort of things she had done? I suppose I may have to report that. And yet, she was so grateful (as well she might be!). It was as if a tremendous stone had been lifted from her shoulders. In my own seeing, she almost appeared to be a new person altogether—the creases in her forehead gone, color in her cheeks, whereas she had been pale and haggard-looking. I know that forgiving another person of their sin is wrong. It's a lie—no one has that power, only God. And yet, to bestow such peace upon another person with just a word! Can he be permitted to make people think that they won't be judged for their sins, that they don't have to make sacrifice for atonement, that violating the law doesn't doom them on the day of judgment? Isn't he putting their souls in jeopardy by giving them false hope? Or is he restoring people to God? I am feeling confused.

Another emergency meeting of the council today. Many spoke about what they had seen and heard of Jesus, the Nazarene. Some were very angry—jealous, almost, it sounded, that some upstart from the countryside was attracting attention. I remained silent. What I could tell them would have added nothing. Except about forgiving the woman, of course. But I'm not ready to tell about that in the council. I think it would be best if I went to speak to Jesus privately, to ask him to explain, to find out what is in his mind and on his heart. He seems approachable. Maybe tonight. After people have gone to their homes, and the streets are quiet. In the dark.

Maybe I should not have gone. My mind is so confused. I began by telling him that I was impressed with what he has been saying and doing. I even told him that I was sure that God was with him—I didn't mean to say that; it just came out. But I guess that's what I've been thinking, in the back of my mind. And then he talked about being born anew. I told him that was ridiculous—no one can emerge twice from the womb! And he talked about being born of water and Spirit. And I guess he didn't mean being born again, but being born in a new way, as it were—to live life on a different level, richer, deeper, less absorbed with one's own ambitions. I think I must have seemed to him a fool, the way I kept bumbling my speech and him asking if I understood or not. How could I be a leader of the people and not know what he was talking about? he asked. But, honestly, I didn't really understand what he was saying, though I sensed that it was vitally important. And even now, I'm not sure I understand what he was saying, but it seems to me even more urgent than it did at the time. I think he was telling me that I need to think about things differently, maybe consider whether God is coming to be present with people in a new way. And people work their own judgment by not coming to the light and allowing themselves to be seen in the light. Belief in the Son of Man who will be lifted up. Having eternal life. Maybe I shouldn't have gone to him at night by myself. Maybe I shouldn't have gone to find him at all. I'm so confused. And yet, I feel as if I'm beginning on some new journey, pushed along it, almost, by a power I've never felt before. I dare not talk of this to the council.

Jesus has left the city. The rumor is that he and his followers from Galilee have gone back out into the country. There was another meeting of the council today, and a general sense of relief that he has gone. And yet, *I don't feel that way. I feel strangely empty.* It was maybe just as well for Jesus, the way some were becoming angry and even starting to voice threats. But I wanted to hear more of his teaching. It's almost as if a light were in the room, and now it's gone.

Jesus is back in town. He has been teaching in the temple. Some people are asking if he might not be the Messiah. That has upset many on the council. The chief priests and some of the Pharisees have ordered him to be arrested if he shows up at the temple again. I fear there's going to be trouble. But why? Because he's speaking the *truth* and people are *repenting*? What are we *coming* to in this country?

The fat is in the fire. Many people are speaking of Jesus as a prophet. Some are going so far as to say with certainty that he is the *Messiah*. Others are ready to believe it, except that it *can't* be so if he comes from *Galilee* and not *Bethlehem*, where *David* was born. The *council* is not going to like that any more than the *Romans* will. But something strange and surprising has happened—something that may anger the chief priests and Pharisees even more. Jesus came back to the temple to teach, and the temple police refused to arrest him. Even they have been won over by his teaching! There was another emergency meeting of the council. This time, I spoke up—I had to! There are people among us who want to have him put to death. And for *what*? For *speaking*? For making *sick* people *well*? I said, "Our law does not judge people without first giving them a hearing to find out what they are doing, does it?" Some accused me of not knowing the scriptures—that the scriptures say nothing about a prophet coming from Galilee! Many others just ignored me. The council meeting was ugly, rancorous. How can people be afraid of the truth?

Almost daily now there are reports of Jesus healing people and teaching and his followers saying he was sent from God, and the chief priests and Pharisees are getting furious. They try to trap him in his own words, but he ends up silencing them and putting them to shame—they end up being caught in their own trap. I hear he has left the city again and gone down to the Jordan. I fear for his safety if he returns to Jerusalem! What is my duty in all this? I am torn.

Word today from Bethany, spreading like flames. Jesus has brought a dead man back to life! That's the report. Impossible, of course! Or is it? The point is, many believe it. I don't know. I'm confused. Never have I known someone so—so free from public opinion or unrestrained by custom. It's almost like what he said that night I talked with him—he's like the wind, just sort of stirring things up by his presence, leaving things changed, though you can't see it, exactly, can't hold it in your hand, can't define it. He's turning things upside down. He's turning *me* upside down—or inside out.

Emergency meeting tonight. Heated debate. Fears about the Romans reacting. Caiaphas said Jesus must die, or the rest of the nation will. I was too scared to speak. Too scared. God help me!

The night before Passover, and rousted out of bed, summoned to the council. Jesus was there, apparently turned in by one of his own followers. The traitor! Caiaphas questioned him; there was a lot of confusion—it was all very rushed. Many accusations. Jesus didn't respond directly. I could not bear to look at him, turned away from him. But it felt like his eyes were fixed on me, boring into my brain. I was scared. I was confused. I don't know what to think anymore. Isn't he saying and doing exactly what the prophets said to say and do? And yet, it's upsetting so many people, seems to violate the fine points of the law. Then they sent him to Pilate, God help him. God help *me*; I'm so confused! I think I know where my duty lies, but don't I have a higher duty *still*? God is with this man. God is *in* this man. There, I've written it. Blasphemy! But how can the truth be blasphemous? O God, forgive me. O God, forgive us all.

Jesus is dead. They crucified him, treated him disgracefully. I feel such a coward. Joseph came and told me—Joseph of Arimathea. Together, we went and asked for the body, to bury it properly. I brought the spices, much more than necessary. I guess I was trying to salve my conscience as I was anointing the body. But he's dead. Nobody can change that. They may expel me from the council for this—probably will. Well, so be it. Never in my whole life have I done anything so . . . daring. Others will say "irresponsible"—befriending a criminal. What's gotten into me? What has made me so reckless? Could it be that I've become a bit like him? "If I have told you about earthly things and you do not believe . . . ," he said to me when I objected that it was impossible to be born a second time. In a way, I feel that

I *have* been born a second time—I mean, I seem to be seeing things differently than I did before I met him, before I heard him speak, before I saw the things that he did. I'm saying things I wouldn't have said before. "And just as Moses lifted up the serpent in the wilderness, so must the Son of Man be lifted up, that whoever believes in him may have eternal life." What, lifted up on a cross? But he's *dead* now, isn't he? No one lives *forever*, do they? At least, not in the world that we can see and touch. There's a knocking on the door, a pounding. I have been summoned by the council. I am to come immediately. God help me. And yet, I am suddenly unafraid. *This* is strange. What has come over me?

Ninth Sunday in Ordinary Time

First Presbyterian Church, Dodge City, Kansas
June 1, 1997

1 Samuel 3:1–10
2 Corinthians 4:5–12
Mark 2:23—3:6

"God Has No Law against Love"

RECENT CONVERSATION AROUND OUR kitchen table has reminded me that there is no stricter legalist than a young child. It is terribly confusing to children to have to try to figure out the rules—when they apply and when they do not. Children do not have the benefit of what years of experience have taught most adults to recognize as "common sense" in the application of rules—which has to do with recognizing what the intended purpose of the rule is. Whenever the Taylors have a chance to sit down for dinner as a family these days, it is almost inevitable that an argument arises over some alleged breach of family duty, some perceived infraction of household procedure, and suddenly the air is thick with rules being quoted and misquoted.

It is not the children's fault, of course. They are just trying to be like adults, who seem to live in a world of rules. And, of course, adults can be pretty strict legalists themselves. As I listen to our budding ten-year-old prosecutor and our seven-year-old defense attorney debating each other across the chicken and biscuits, it strikes me that it is a wonder how *any* child can make sense of our rule-bound world. It is *full* of legal and ethical dilemmas. How many times do parents hear what-ifs from their children? It is their way of creating some sense of justice out of laws that they perceive are sometimes contradictory, rules that are sometimes at odds with each other and with higher truths that no law can reduce to words. A child hears from her mother that we must always be kind to animals. The same child hears from her father that we must always obey the rules. Walking to school along the sidewalk one day, the child sees a kitten fall from a tree onto the lawn beneath. The kitten tries to stand up, and cannot—it is obviously injured. Compassion floods the child's soul, and her first impulse is to rush to the kitten to comfort it and take it to the veterinarian. But between the sidewalk and the tree is a sign that says, in big letters, "Keep Off the Grass."

Let's raise the stakes. A man is traveling along a road, and sees another man lying in a ditch, his clothes torn and his face bruised and his hands bloodied. It is clear from his clothing that the injured man is someone whose nationality and religion forbid him to have any contact with the traveler. Besides, there is danger to the traveler—the perpetrators of *this* crime might be lurking nearby, ready to assault their *next* victim, or perhaps it is no crime at all, but a setup; the law of custom and the law of self-preservation are pitted against the law of compassion.

And now a third case: Jesus was teaching in a synagogue one sabbath, and among those gathered there were some of his enemies, eager to find fault with him. Jesus knew that they were there, but he also saw in the crowd a man who had a withered hand, weak and limp. Jesus was well aware that the literal words of the laws of Moses forbade healing on the sabbath, but Jesus told the man to stretch out his hand, and immediately his hand was restored to soundness. "Is it lawful to do good or to do harm on the sabbath, to save life or to kill?" (Mark 3:4 NRSV) Jesus had asked his opponents before the man's hand was restored. And when they saw what had happened, "[t]he Pharisees went out and immediately conspired with the Herodians against him, how to destroy him" (3:6 NRSV). They were ready to pounce as soon as Jesus took a misstep. *They* had the law of the *sabbath* on *their* side, very specific and very detailed: You shall do no work on the sabbath, because the Lord God rested on the seventh day and commands *us* to rest as well. *Jesus* had the law of *compassion* on *his* side, very general and very simple: "You shall love your neighbor as yourself" (12:31 NRSV). And the Pharisees hated him for it. Hatred makes strange bedfellows—in this instance, these righteous defenders of the law and the standards and the traditions of the Jewish faith entered league with supporters of a king who cared *nothing* about the law and the standards and the traditions of the Jewish faith, and they set about to have Jesus killed.

By the common measure, these Pharisees were not bad people. Indeed, they were highly admired in their society as model citizens, counted as righteous men—if sometimes *self*-righteous—recognized as champions of religion, alert against immorality, warning against relaxing the standards of their tradition. We have no reason for thinking that they kicked dogs or cursed children. But they were overly impressed with the word of the law and irrationally jealous of Jesus, and it was easy for them, when they saw the opportunity of attacking Jesus on the *basis* of the *law*, to ignore the *good* that he was doing. They felt threatened—their institutions and their traditions and their own prestige—and suddenly, all that *mattered* was keeping the rules, obeying the law to the *letter*. They might have recognized in some other case that institutions and traditions and personal prestige are not as important as serving human beings in need, but when their own interests were involved, they did not notice that they had swallowed a camel while straining on a gnat.

What is it about people—especially religious people—that we are so willing sometimes to let the defense of some favorite principle blind us to our total violation of the simplest truth? We engage in long debates that consume our energy and monopolize our interest and divert our resources away from mission, away from doing what Jesus commanded us to do. For the sake of purity of doctrine and practice, some of our Christian forebears burned other Christians at the stake. For the sake of purity of doctrine and practice, some of our fellow contemporary Christians in recent years, even fellow Presbyterians, have not scrupled to slander their religious opponents and destroy their careers. When the debating instinct gets the upper hand over love—when we cease to live for the purpose of doing good for others because we are so obsessed with winning on some principle of doctrine or practice—then our religion is dead. Then we have become more interested in scoring our point than in caring for what happens to other people and to the world and even to the gospel. "[Y]ou will know them by their fruits" (Matt 7:20 NRSV). Too often in Christian history and in modern church infighting, the fruits by which Christians are best known are the wreckage of split congregations, shrinking denominations, crippled mission, and thicker and thicker books of rules. And our Lord in heaven must shake his head and weep that his own followers are so susceptible to the same prejudice and pride and hatred that put him on the cross. Burning a heretic does no honor to Christ. Hounding dedicated church administrators out of office does nothing to advance the gospel. Putting the strict word of the law *above* practical and nonjudgmental expressions of love does not please God.

Jesus said to the Pharisees, "'Is it lawful to do *good* or to do *harm* on the sabbath, to *save* life or to *kill*?' But they were silent" (Mark 3:4 NRSV). The reason they were silent is that, *of course*, it is *lawful* to do *good* and *un*lawful to do *harm*, lawful to save a life, and therefore to heal, *whenever*, even on the *sabbath*. Any regulations against healing on the sabbath went far beyond the intention behind the law against working on the seventh day. God is the God of mercy, and God delights to have people healed. Love is doing good for another person, and God has no law against love. The Son of Man is Lord of the sabbath—Jesus Christ—and Jesus Christ is all about healing and wholeness and forgiveness and redemption. The day on which God was worshiped was a perfectly appropriate time for restoring the man's hand, even though it was in no way a life-or-death situation for the man, because restoring the man's hand, making him *whole* again, was an act of *love*. So Jesus proceeded to heal him, because it is *never* appropriate to do *evil*, and to *refuse* to do *good* is the same thing as doing *evil*. Not to *heal* when you have the ability to do so is the same thing as committing injury. Not *forgiving* is the same thing as condemning to hell. The Pharisees didn't see it that way; their interest at that point was not in God's love for the afflicted man, but in Jesus' challenge to their tradition and their institutions and their prestige. "[Jesus] looked around at them with anger; he was grieved at their hardness of heart and said to the man, 'Stretch out your hand.' He stretched it out, and his hand was restored" (3:5b–c NRSV).

This is one of only two places in the Gospel where Jesus is described as being angry—a pretty harsh word in Greek. He was resentful at the inhumanity of these guardians of the law and the tradition—at their bigotry and fanaticism, their irrational hatred of him and their indifference to the suffering of others. They had elevated themselves above responsibility for responding to human need; their correct doctrine and their ethical purity insulated them from simple human compassion that knows no boundary of religious orthodoxy. The sabbath law, Jesus declared, was grounded in human welfare; how could anyone presume to use it to *obstruct* someone's well-being? Every legalism that makes obedience a *burden* is a slander against the redeeming purpose of God. How could the Pharisees or anyone else blaspheme God by suggesting that he would have any law against love?

If the Pharisees that day had had any love for the person afflicted with an infirmity, if they had had any love for God, they would have responded to the miracle of healing not with cold hostility and vengeful conspiracy, but with amazement and joy. They should have been *grateful* for the wondrous ways of God. It should have strengthened their faith. Instead, they plotted to destroy God's Son. Are there miracles of God's love happening in our midst today that are being criticized because they seem to go beyond the laws by which faith is guarded against impurity, against disorder, against spontaneity? Is the inclusive invitation of Christ sometimes muted by claims of privilege and prestige? Is the simple human response of compassion sometimes forbidden by fears of contamination? Are people being newly awakened to faith only then to find themselves shut out of the faith community because of class or race or nationality or condition? Are people's *real needs* being *neglected* because the rules make it easy to rationalize away our ministering to them in practical and costly ways?

There are so many rules in our world, so many competing and conflicting voices of authority, that we can spend a lot of time justifying our actions or our inactions, even by claiming that it is for the sake of religious purity, of defending God. But that is not what being a Christian is about. Surely, as Jesus himself demonstrated, God has no law against love.

Tenth Sunday in Ordinary Time

First Presbyterian Church, Dodge City, Kansas
June 5, 1994

1 Samuel 8:4-20; 11:14-15
2 Corinthians 4:13—5:1
Mark 3:20-35 (GNT)

"And They Said, 'He's Gone Mad!'"

It may seem rather strange, but, although I remember every one of my elementary and junior and senior high school teachers by name and face, I can recall only one of my church school teachers. It was at First Presbyterian Church in El Paso, Texas, and it must have been about fourth grade. She was a middle-aged woman who had had an interesting life—she used to tell us stories about experiences in the South American country of Chile, where she and her geologist husband had lived for a time. But that is not why I remember her so well. She had an unusual name—Mrs. Duisberg—and some of the other children used to make fun of her name, as children will. But that is not why I remember her so well. The reason that I remember her so well is that every two or three weeks I would get a telephone call from her in the evening, asking whether I had done my Bible-reading devotional for the day yet—we used to have a daily Bible-reading curriculum called "Day by Day with My Bible." The truth is, I was very faithful to attend church school, but not very faithful to read the daily lessons. "No, Mrs. Duisberg, I haven't done it yet for today." Then, in a manner and tone of voice that had not a trace of judgmentalism or criticism in it, Mrs. Duisberg would say, "Why don't we do it together on the telephone?" And I would go and get my Bible and the lesson, and we would spend twenty or thirty minutes on the telephone together. As I said, this would happen every two or three weeks—I never seemed to learn—and since there were perhaps thirty children in my church school class, and I know that I was not at all the only one who did not do the assignment without her nudging, my teacher must have spent an average of an hour or more on the telephone every weeknight calling and doing the lesson with us or asking us questions about it. And of all my church school teachers, Mrs. Duisberg is the one I remember. And what I remember is her devotion. And I suppose that the children who made fun of her name were also, in some degree, making fun of her devotion. None of us, and probably none of our parents, had ever run into a church school teacher who would spend that much time and effort, far beyond what was necessary to prepare well for Sunday morning's class. Why would anyone devote so much precious time and thoughtful effort to the task of passing on the faith to the next generation? Who would have thought that teaching church school was that important? What was she, crazy? I remember Mrs. Duisberg.

Faithfulness—true faithfulness—is a rare commodity. Seeking first and always to do the will of God, whatever the cost to one's leisure time, whatever the cost to one's family time, whatever the cost to one's popularity, whatever the cost to one's reputation, whatever the cost to one's bank account, is uncommon. And yet, that is what God expects of us, and that is what Jesus modeled for his church. Our devotion to the purpose of God and the command of Christ should be so radical, as individuals and as a congregation, that other people—even other people who regard themselves as Christians—may well conclude that we've gone mad.

We do not have to read very far into Mark's Gospel before we discover that Jesus himself, in his faithful devotion to God, was considered by many people to be insane. He had rid a man of an evil spirit that possessed him, and healed Simon's mother-in-law and many others who were sick with disease, and had driven out many demons from them, had reached out and touched a man afflicted with leprosy—unthinkable by common standards of hygiene and churchly propriety, much like the way some people think of AIDS today—had healed a paralytic and restored a withered hand, had answered those who criticized his disciples because they satisfied their hunger by eating daily and by picking grain on the sabbath (falling under the category of "We don't do that sort of thing in this church"). Those *outside* the old order were eager to hear his preaching and to be healed by his touch—a large crowd even followed him home one day, and petitioned him so to teach and preach and heal that he and his disciples did not even have time for dinner.

People were talking. Jesus' family—his mother and brothers and sisters—heard about how he was breaking the rules, the normal way of doing things, with his easy display of grace, and in a combination of love and embarrassment, "they set out to take charge of him, because people were saying, 'He's gone mad!'" (Mark 3:21b GNT). Jesus was accomplishing results for the kingdom of God; he was doing good, but people in authority seemed blind to all that and distrustful of him—blinded by their power and their traditions, distrustful of his sincere goodness and quick forgiveness. Cruel irony! His very dedication to God's will, his total faithfulness to God's purpose, opened him to criticism from the old guard that he was possessed by the devil. It seemed to them that he was determined to stir up trouble, when all he was doing was living out the good news. And *others* thought that he was out of his mind. It seemed to *them* that he was investing his time and talents in people and in ministry in a way that no reasonable person would do. They were very nearly calling the good that he was accomplishing and demonstrating for others "evil," and so they were dangerously close to committing the one unforgiveable sin.

Faithful ministry often garners human scorn rather than human praise. Those who seek to live out the good news frequently attract severe criticism. Consider Paul, who in several of his letters was having to defend himself against scurrilous rumors and mean charges against his integrity as a human being and his authority as an apostle. Unfortunately, we are not privileged to have full accounts of what had produced the factionalism in some of the churches he founded or the exact words or behavior that prompted the complaints against him. Judging from what sometimes happens to devoted ministers and laypeople in churches in our own day, it was probably a mixture of his trying to be faithful to his calling to proclaim gospel truths while seeking to be pastoral rather than confrontational, reminding the libertines of divine law and reminding the legalists of divine grace, and reminding everyone of the need to be good stewards of the rich treasure God had placed in their care. That was certainly enough to earn Paul the dissatisfaction of some congregation members. At Corinth, where the church had been factionalized almost from the beginning, it seems that Paul had been accused of acting deceptively in some manner, and of misrepresenting the word of God to suit his own purposes. Some of the Corinthian Christians, no doubt, thought that he was ignoring Old Testament law when he preached against the hazards of judgmental legalism, which is the sin of pride. Undoubtedly, some mistook his earnest zeal for Christ as a lack of humor or individual concern. Unquestionably, some who found the truth offensive simply avoided self-examination by dismissing the messenger. What, had he gone mad? Paul certainly suffered contempt and rebuke, according to his letters and the book of Acts. But his love of the church and the people in it, and his faith in the promises of God and the lordship of Christ, compelled him to carry on, and even to regard affliction as preparing him and others in similar circumstances for an everlasting glory beyond human imagining, "because we look not at what can be seen but at what cannot be seen; for what can be seen is temporary, but what cannot be seen is eternal" (2 Cor 4:18 NRSV).

If Paul had not spoken over and over again his belief in the gospel as all-important, as a claim upon every aspect of every life, he would never have been persecuted or perplexed. But in that event, the Corinthians would never have been given hope of being raised with Christ. Paul felt a deep responsibility for those whom God had placed in his spiritual charge. Their understanding of Christ and their response to Christ's command could not be a matter of indifference to him. If, by their quarrelsome behavior or even their slanderous rumors about him and vocal dissatisfactions with him, they demonstrated a failure to grasp the fundamental implications of the gospel for faithful living, then he must subject himself to the persecution all the more to give witness to the crucified and risen Christ. Finally, as Paul neared the end of his career as an apostle, he was arrested, and the provincial governor, Festus, brought him before King Agrippa to state his case.

> "Wherefore, O King Agrippa, I was not disobedient to the heavenly vision, but declared first to those at Damascus, then at Jerusalem and throughout all the country of Judea, and also to the Gentiles, that they should repent and turn to God and perform deeds worthy of their repentance. For this reason the Jews seized me in the temple and tried to kill me. To this day I have had the help that comes from God, and so I stand here testifying to both small and great, saying nothing but what the prophets and Moses said would come to pass: that the Christ must suffer, and that, by being the first to rise from the dead, he would proclaim light both to the people and to the Gentiles."
>
> And as he thus made his defense, Festus [the governor] said with a loud voice, "Paul, you are mad . . . ." "I am not mad, most excellent Festus, but I am speaking the truth." (Acts 26:19–24b, 25 RSV)

I have often wondered whether my church school teacher was aware that some of the children were making fun of her dedication, and whether that motivated her all the more to devote her evenings and Sundays to our nurture in the Christian faith. Was she mad to spend so much time and energy and, I am quite sure, prayer, on a bunch of unappreciative fourth-graders—many of whom, even at that age, before adolescent activities or adult responsibilities, wouldn't take twenty minutes a day to read their

Bible? Certainly, her spirit was very much akin to Paul's, and, I believe, not far from Christ's.

Mark uses stories such as our Gospel reading this morning to raise questions about who Jesus is for his readers. Mark had already told of many instances of Jesus healing and caring and teaching and preaching. And then he tells us, "[P]eople were saying, 'He's gone mad!'" (Mark 3:21b GNT). Mark is asking us: Was Jesus mad? Was Jesus possessed by the devil? Did Jesus have an evil spirit in him? Or was Jesus the way, the truth, and the life?

Do some of the people around us think that we're crazy for believing and acting upon the promises of God, for trying to govern every part of our lives by Christ's command, for advocating sharing God's blessings in *trust* of his providence rather than hoarding them out of fear that he may not be provident tomorrow, for testifying that *God's purpose* can never be achieved by using the *devil's means*, for giving witness that *no* person is ever beyond the boundless reaches of God's love and mercy except the one who calls the good work of the Holy Spirit "evil"? Is Mark perhaps suggesting that if no one has ever called *us* "mad," then perhaps we should question how faithful we are being to Christ? "He's gone mad!" or "She's gone mad!" may be the ultimate tribute to a person who knows not two masters, but only one—God in Jesus Christ.

Eleventh Sunday in Ordinary Time

Spanish Springs Presbyterian Church, Sparks, Nevada
June 14, 2009

1 Samuel 15:34—16:13
2 Corinthians 5:6–10, 14–17
Mark 4:26–34

"To See Aright"

TODAY'S FIRST READING IS about Samuel's anointing of David to be king over Israel. The story told in these verses is important, and many of us know about it. But we can't appreciate its full significance without backing up a little bit to the anointing of David's *predecessor, Saul,* which was *also* performed by Samuel.

Recall that the people of Israel, who had been ruled by leaders whom the Bible refers to as "judges" (though settling *disputes* among people was only *one* of their functions), eventually decided that they wanted to be like all the *other* nations around them. They wanted a *king.* Samuel, who was then serving as judge over Israel, reported the clamoring of the people to the Lord, and the Lord told Samuel to warn the people what having a king would mean. They would *indeed* become like all the nations around them. A king would send their sons off to war and press them into labor in his fields and would take their daughters and make them serve in his household. He would confiscate the best of their lands and parcel them out as spoil for his patronage system. He would tax them by taking a tenth of their flocks and they would end up being essentially slaves to the system that would support the royal lifestyle.

Samuel faithfully told the people what the Lord had said. "But the people refused to listen to the voice of Samuel; they said, 'No! but we are determined to have a king over us, so that we also may be like other nations'"

(1 Sam 8:19–20a NRSV). Samuel reported back to the Lord his inability to dissuade the people from having a king. And the Lord, rather than argue the point, told Samuel to go ahead and *give* them a king. And the Lord sent to Samuel from the land of Benjamin a young man, handsome and tall—the tallest in the land, apparently—and told Samuel to anoint him as king. The boy's name was Saul, and the Lord said that he would be the one who would save the Israelites from the Philistines. So Samuel anointed Saul as king as the Lord directed him, and Saul defeated several of Israel's enemies, and eventually his son, Jonathan, helped defeat the Philistines as well.

But Saul did not follow the Lord's commands in battle, and he proved to be too indulgent of his wayward children. "And the LORD was sorry that he had made Saul king over Israel" (15:35b NRSV)—regardless of his handsome features and his imposing stature. And the Lord gave Samuel a new mission: "'I will send you to Jesse the Bethlehemite, for I have provided for myself a king among his sons'" (16:1c NRSV). And, as we read today, Samuel summoned Jesse to parade all of his sons before him. And Samuel thought surely Jesse's son Eliab was the one the Lord wanted as king. "But the LORD said to Samuel, 'Do not look on his appearance or on the height of his stature'"—the very characteristics that seemed to qualify *Saul* as the Lord's choice the *last* time around—"'because I have rejected him; for the LORD does not see as mortals see; they look on the outward appearance, but the LORD looks on the heart'" (16:7 NRSV). And so it went with each of the seven young men Jesse summoned into Samuel's presence—seven, the number that represents completeness—but the Lord rejected them all. "Samuel said to Jesse, 'Are *all* your sons here?' And [Jesse] said, 'There remains yet the youngest, but he is keeping the sheep'" (16:11 NRSV). So David was summoned from the flocks—that ought to tell us something, for what Israel *really* needed was a *shepherd*—and, lo and behold, he too was handsome, but apparently not so strong and tall as Saul had been, or as his own brothers, for that matter. And Samuel anointed him king. And in the very next chapter, it was little *David*, child number *eight*, the *leftover*, armed only with his *slingshot*—not Saul, tall of stature and encased in all his armor—who felled the Philistine giant Goliath. And David went on to be the greatest of Israel's kings, the one alongside whom all the others would be judged, the one through whom it was so important for the evangelists to reckon the lineage of Jesus, the good shepherd, put to death by the authorities because some hailed him as king of the Jews, but raised by God in one great divine verdict of "Yes" on all that he had said and done.

Much later, *another* Saul, a Pharisee, himself had a very human standard for judging people, it seems, and when he sized up Jesus, who had been crucified as a blasphemer and an insurrectionist, he counted him an enemy of God. What he saw was a lawbreaker who encouraged *others* to disregard the law. But then the risen Lord took away Saul's vision, and Saul became aware that Jesus was in fact the Christ, God's Messiah, David's true successor. And Saul's name was changed to Paul, and Paul came to realize that no one should make judgments on the basis of human standards of what is good and right and successful. "From now on, therefore, we regard no one from a human point of view; even though we once knew Christ from a human point of view, we know him no longer in that way" (2 Cor 5:16 NRSV). No longer was Jesus just a carpenter's son from an unimpressive little town in the hills of Galilee. No longer was Jesus just another teacher and healer. No longer was Jesus just another challenger of the status quo whom Rome dealt with brutally and decisively, proof that kindness and mercy and generosity all identify one as a pathetic loser in the game of life. There was a *new* standard in the world. "So if anyone is in Christ, there is a new creation: everything old has passed away; see, everything has become new" (5:17 NRSV)! To all appearance, the cross was a sign of God's rejection, God's abandonment, God's judgment. But "the LORD does not see as mortals see; they look on the outward appearance, but the LORD looks on the heart" (1 Sam 16:7b NRSV). To see aright requires looking at people, at situations, at history, at opportunities, through *God's* eyes.

It seems that that was no easier to do in ancient times than it is today, and it was no easier for Jesus' original disciples to do than it is for Jesus' modern disciples. We even tend to judge the effectiveness of the church, or of a congregation, or of a program of ministry, on the world's terms of success rather than on God's scale of faithfulness. And, apparently, the same was true even in the earliest days of the Christian movement. And if Samuel had given in to his very human first impression, he would have anointed as king not *God's* chosen one, but the one who happened to fit *human* preconceptions—*Eliab*, not *David*. And he would have made a *mistake*. *God's* choice was the *outsider*, the *least* impressive, the little boy not strong enough or big enough to be useful around the house or to do a man's job. *He* played *music*. *He* wrote *poetry*. While *other* young men practiced with the javelin and the spear, *he* practiced the lyre and occasionally toyed with a slingshot. Later in life, his military genius would expand the borders of Israel and his political insight would unite disparate tribes into a mighty nation and his religious devotion would persuade a people to bow down to God. But when we first meet him in the Bible, when Samuel first saw him in the mudroom of Jesse's farmhouse, he was not yet a genius or a politician or the spiritual conscience of *anyone*. But *God* could see in him *all* these things, and, fortunately for the history of salvation, Samuel trusted *God's* judgment above his *own*.

What most impresses God is hardly ever what most impresses human beings. Sometimes, even those who would follow *Jesus* become impatient with God's standards of success, certainly with God's timetable of fulfillment. All through his ministry, people were attracted to Jesus only to become disappointed that he wouldn't bend to their agenda, and so they drifted away. The crowd that greeted him on Palm Sunday is popularly thought to have turned against him on Good Friday, or at least to have lost their enthusiasm for him by the end of the week. Very few stuck with him all the way to the crucifixion—the needful event in the salvation of humankind. In Mark's Gospel, none at all of the Twelve remained faithful to Jesus, unable to believe that his death was the route to God's kingdom. He had tried to tell them many times, of course, and they would sort of nod but never quite comprehend. And so, when their faithfulness would have counted the most, they had given up on Jesus' promises and had given in to the world's assessment, or the assessment of Pharisees, like Paul had once been. And they very nearly missed the news of the resurrection, very nearly missed the birth of the church.

"With what can we compare the kingdom of God, or what parable will we use for it?" Jesus once asked them. "It is like a mustard seed, which, when sown upon the ground, is the smallest of all the seeds on earth; yet when it is sown it grows up and becomes the greatest of all shrubs, and puts forth large branches, so that the birds of the air can make nests in its shade" (Mark 4:30–32 NRSV). Someone recently asked me, "What are you doing in such a small church?" Well, in fact, we have more people in worship here on a Sunday morning than in half the churches of our denomination. And I remember that 130-some church members, and their children, and other regular attenders and participants, make up a Presbyterian church in Spanish Springs, where ten and a half years ago there *was* no Presbyterian church, and I remember the importance to me of each of those people, you, and your importance to God. The simple answer is, I was called here before there was a single member, before there was a single worshiper, when as yet Spanish Springs Presbyterian Church wouldn't even have qualified as a mustard seed.

Even in the midst of long odds, opposition, and difficulty, Jesus told his disciples, the end result for seed sown for the sake of the kingdom of God is assured. It needs human tending. It requires human effort. But ultimately, the growth rests with God, whose field of vision is far broader than any human perspective, whose verdict of success rests on a measurement far truer than any human standard, who examines the human heart in search of faith. As far as people like Pontius Pilate were concerned, the cross was an unambiguous sign of *failure*. The faithfulness of God to his purpose of redemption transformed the cross into a sign of *triumph*. Today, even non-Christians universally recognize it as the cherished symbol for a third of the world's population—those whose holy scriptures declare, "From now on, therefore, we regard no one from a human point of view; even though we once knew Christ from a human point of view, we know him no longer in that way" (2 Cor 5:16 NRSV). What does that say about us? "[I]f anyone is in Christ, there is a new creation: everything old has passed away; see, everything has become new" (5:17 NRSV)!

Long ago, when Israel's very first king, strong and tall and everyone's picture of a champion, fell short of God's hopes, a new ruler was anointed according to God's intention—not by historical accident, not by political maneuvering, not by popular vote, not according to worldly criteria. By human estimation, he was the least likely to be God's choice to replace Saul. Even the prophet Samuel would have settled for one, perhaps *any* one, of his *brothers*. Height, muscles, interest in the things that kings were commonly thought to be interested in—all these characteristics favored someone *other* than David, militated *against* David. "'I cannot walk with these,'" David said when Saul dressed him up in helmet and armor and sword, "'for I am not used to them'" (1 Sam 17:39b NRSV). "'It is not for these things that I was chosen by God.'" "So David removed them. Then he took his staff in his hand, and chose five smooth stones from the wadi, and put them in his shepherd's bag, in the pouch; his sling was in his hand, and he drew near to the Philistine. . . . David said to the Philistine, 'You come to me with sword and spear and javelin; but I come to you in the name of the Lord of hosts, the God of the armies of Israel, whom you have defied'" (17:39c–40, 45 NRSV). You know the rest of the story.

Twelfth Sunday in Ordinary Time

Spanish Springs Presbyterian Church, Sparks, Nevada
June 19, 2006

1 Samuel 17:1a, 4–11, 19–23, 32–49
2 Corinthians 6:1–13
Mark 4:35–41

"God on Board"

THE LECTIONARY FOR THIS morning gives us two vivid stories that fill the imagination of every Sunday school child and confound the logic of every sophisticated adult—the tale of little David, who felled the armor-clad Philistine giant Goliath, and a tale of Jesus, who, with a word, stilled wind and wave. They had very different settings, these two stories, but they both speak strongly of the might of God, and of the importance of trusting in the purpose of God. In an age when the speed of communications vastly outpaces our understanding of events, in an era when news of what's in bottled water or hot dogs grabs headlines around the country and has telephones ringing off the hook on talk shows, in a time when sensationalized reports of economic actions taken by a religious denomination in response to provocative acts in the Middle East can result in a drastic decrease in giving to support the church, it is important for us to remember and ponder the *power* of God, which *cannot* be enfeebled, and the *purpose* of God, which *cannot* be thwarted, and the fact that *God's* rule ultimately depends *not* upon *our* poor fretting and sweating, but upon God being God.

You remember how, out of the camp of the Philistines, there came up to fight in a duel to settle the war between them and the Israelites a champion, a huge man covered with armor and bearing javelin and spear, a blustering bully, really, whose appearance and whose braggadocio terrified the Israelites and their king, Saul. You will remember that the Israelites had petitioned Samuel the prophet to ask God for a king, that they might be like the other nations, and that their king might fight their battles for them. But things weren't working out that way. The king panicked along with his army in the face of the Philistine's challenge. Not a one of Saul's soldiers would offer to defend Israel by going against Goliath. And then came along a little shepherd lad who was carrying provisions, at his father's behest, to his older brothers, who were soldiers in the king's army, and when the shepherd boy saw the Israelites and the Philistines lined up for battle, he entrusted the supplies to the baggage handler and ran up to the battle line to greet his brothers, and there heard Goliath the big Philistine once more lay down his challenge. And "David said to the men who stood by him, 'What shall be done for the man who kills this Philistine, and takes away the reproach from Israel? For who is this uncircumcised Philistine that he should defy the armies of the living God?" (1 Sam 17:26 NRSV).

It seems that, in their fright at seeing Goliath and in their willingness to suffer his taunting insults, Saul and his troops had *forgotten* about being the army of the living God, about God's covenant with Israel, about God's promises to Abraham and Sarah, about God's purpose that Israel, far from being *annihilated*, would *endure* and would be a blessing to all humankind. But when Saul heard about David's speech, he sent for the boy, and David said to his king, "'Let no one's heart fail because of *him*; your servant will go and fight with this Philistine'" (17:32 NRSV). Saul, probably as much *amused* as *amazed*, objected that David was just a boy, and Goliath was a veritable fighting machine, but David answered that he had tracked and killed lions and bears that had menaced his father's sheep. And "David said, 'The LORD, who saved me from the paw of the lion and from the paw of the bear, will save me from the hand of this Philistine'" (17:37a NRSV). And Saul was persuaded to let David battle Goliath. Missing the depth of David's faith, the king outfitted him with his own cumbersome armor, which must have been much too big and much too heavy for the boy. "'I cannot walk with these'" (17:39b NRSV), David said of the armor, which is the equipment that the *nations* use to fight battles. He took it all off, and instead put five river pebbles in his shepherd's pouch, and, with his slingshot in his hand, went off to meet the Philistine. And when the Philistine saw who it was that the Israelites had sent against him, a mere youth, he cursed David and heaped scorn upon him. But, undaunted, David answered, "'You come to me with sword and spear and javelin; but I come to *you* in the name of the LORD of hosts, the God of the armies of Israel, whom you have defied. This very day the LORD will deliver you into my hand, and I will strike you down and cut off your head'" (17:45–46a NRSV). And as the contemptuous Philistine drew close, David pulled out a stone from his bag and slung it at

Goliath, and Goliath fell to the ground, and all who were present and all who heard about it saw the power of the God of Israel, who can bring down the mighty with a pebble.

Earlier in the book, the Lord had directed Samuel the prophet to anoint Saul to be prince over his people Israel that he might *deliver* them from the hand of the Philistines. And yet, when the Philistine threat *materialized* in the form of *Goliath*, Saul retreated with the rest and cowered before the big warrior, disregarding God's promise and forgetting his divine commission, and Israel was intimidated into immobility. Death, wreck, and destruction were the only possibilities they saw before them—the end of Israel, the end of themselves. But *God's* purpose would *not* be defeated, though Israel was finally saved not by a massive army and bristling weapons, but by a little boy with a slingshot who believed in the faithfulness of God.

Jesus had called to himself twelve to be with him and to go out and preach and to have authority, Mark tells us, to cast out all sorts of demons. And yet, not long after, when they were all together in a boat, and a storm came up and the boat seemed in danger of being capsized by the demons of the deep, they *forgot* the authority Jesus had given them and even accused their slumbering Master of having no regard for their safety, of ignoring their storm-tossed plight. "[Jesus] woke up and rebuked the wind, and said to the sea, 'Peace! Be still!' Then the wind ceased, and there was a dead calm. He said to them, 'Why are you afraid? Have you still no faith?'" (Mark 4:39–40 NRSV). And, we might suppose, he went back to sleep. "And they were filled with great awe and said to one another, 'Who then is this, that even the wind and the sea obey him?'" (4:41 NRSV). We, as Mark's readers, know the answer, and *why* demons of all sorts—human, superhuman, and *in*human—must submit and fall silent before Jesus: he is Christ, who has all the authority and power of God.

The disciples did not seem to understand that they had God on board the boat with them that night. They had, by then, heard Jesus teach many times. But, from their passive point of view, everything that he said remained in the realm of *theory*—nice thoughts and fine speech. They had not yet ever had to *practice* the faith of which Jesus taught. And so far, of course, they had remained on firm and familiar ground. But then, at Christ's bidding, they went out on the lake together—a place away from the security of town and countryside, a place notorious for sudden storms, a place of risk, a place where they were vulnerable. When a tempest arose, they thought that all that kept them from total annihilation was their own wits and worry, and neither of *them* appeared up to the *task*. The same was true of Saul when he saw what he thought was a hopeless contest between his army and the military prowess of the Philistines.

It is strange that, two thousand years after the resurrection of Jesus—God's mighty triumph in what seemed the most hopeless case possible—we are just as susceptible, both as individuals and as a civilization, and even as Christ's church, to being whipped into hand-wringing timidity by almost any crisis. "Why are you afraid?" Jesus asked the panicked disciples into whose hands he would eventually place the future of his ministry. "Have you still no faith?" (4:40 NRSV). "[W]ho is this uncircumcised Philistine that *he* should defy the armies of the living *God*?" (1 Sam 17:26b NRSV)David rhetorically demanded to know.

Perhaps it is because there have been so many instances in history of kings and generals presuming upon the unqualified coincidence between their desires and God's will that Christians today seem to feel the threat of total destruction in every perilous wind and every intimidating wave. Books and movies have delved into this theological question, offering us scenes of some officer on one side of the battle lines, discouraged by unfavorable weather and other things going wrong, saying to himself, "Sometimes, I wonder just whose side God is on." And after that, an officer in the opposing forces on the other side of the battle lines, discouraged by the unpreparedness of his superiors and other things going wrong, says to *him*self, "Sometimes, I wonder just whose side God is on."

Military victory, of course, does not prove God's favor, nor even calm winds and quiet seas. The *Axis* powers certainly won an impressive number of battles during the course of World War II, and without the thunderstorms that can cause millions of dollars in damage with wind and hail, some crops in "America's Breadbasket" would never get any moisture at all. Is God's purpose in the victory of our enemy, and the death of innocent men, women, and children? Is it God's intention to destroy one person's crop, and home and school and church, just in order that *another* person's crop might be *watered*? We have learned to be cautious about reading God's will in every disaster and every bit of good fortune. But without some conviction that God wills the *good*, and that *life* and *peace* and *mercy* and *compassion* are good, we would be daunted into such paralyzing inaction that evil would always have an easy way of it in the world. And without *acting* upon that conviction, without standing up against the Philistines of *our* day that threaten to ravage God's world, then the demons that Christ promises must fall silent to the will of God will in fact go unexorcised and will have freedom to scour the landscape and terrorize humankind and destroy much that could be saved. And I am not speaking only or even primarily about military action, but standing up against the assumptions and presumptions that have fouled the environment, that are widening the gap between rich and poor, that are dehumanizing us at every turn. Without *acting* upon our faith, without courageously persisting in steering the bow of our ship toward the destination to which Christ points us, our discipleship will either end up wrecked on the rocks of what appear to worldly human eyes to be towering impossibilities but which God is prepared to demolish with the smallest pebble from our slingshot, or our discipleship will find itself beached high, dry, and irrelevant upon the sterile sands of financial security and passionless comfort.

People of faith: God is on board our little boat! God proved himself bigger and stronger even than mighty Goliath, and while all the armed host of Israel trembled, a little shepherd boy, trusting in the living God, brought down the fearsome giant with a pebble. God is on board our little boat! The same Jesus Christ who summons us with the words "'Let us go across to the other side'" (Mark 4:35b NRSV) is with us even on the stormiest night. "'Peace! Be still!'" said Jesus. "Then the wind ceased, and there was a dead calm. He said to them, 'Why are you afraid? Have you still no faith?'" (4:39b–40 NRSV).

The great issues of our day, the great disappointments of our lives, may seem staggering in complexity, may seem insoluble within the limits of human imagination and human resources. But if God's purpose of goodness, of redemption, of renewal, of hope is bound up in them, then we are not *limited* to *human* imagination and *human* resources. "And [the disciples] were filled with great awe and said to one another, 'Who then is this, that even the wind and the sea obey him?'" (4:41 NRSV). In every good and worthy effort, in every true and faithful task, in every fine and obedient work, we have God on board.

Thirteenth Sunday in Ordinary Time

Spanish Springs Presbyterian Church, Sparks, Nevada
June 29, 2003

2 Samuel 1:1, 17–27
2 Corinthians 8:7–15
Mark 5:21–43

"The Priorities of God"

IT MUST HAVE SEEMED to the disciples to be a great opportunity, though they were undoubtedly tired and probably overwhelmed by the crowd that gathered around them immediately when they stepped out of the boat in which they had crossed the Sea of Galilee. The common people had heard of Jesus' miracles, and they thronged into the street to greet him as soon as word spread that he had come to their town.

Jesus had not found such an enthusiastic welcome in the synagogues, where the Pharisees watched him critically and spoke of him with contempt. Indeed, it was when Jesus cured a man with a withered hand at a synagogue that the Pharisees joined with the supporters of King Herod to conspire against him. But now, one of the *leaders* of a synagogue, an important and honored figure in the community, a man named Jairus, undoubtedly one of the wealthiest and most influential people in the whole town, came up to Jesus as his boat landed, and, abandoning etiquette and ignoring protocol, he fell down at Jesus' feet and begged him to come heal his critically ill daughter with his touch. *Finally*, some *recognition* of Jesus' *powers*! *Finally*, some *respect* for Jesus' *authority*! *Finally*, some *headway* among respectable people who could make a *difference* in the official attitude toward Jesus and his ministry! The disciples had already seen miracles of people being healed of all sorts of diseases. Surely Jesus could cure yet one more, and send his stock price soaring, so to speak, at the same time. They must have felt renewed vigor in spite of their fatigue. Things were looking up. Their work was paying off. They started up in the direction of Jairus' house.

But then, something unforeseen happened. A woman, considered unclean and untouchable, came up behind Jesus and reached out to touch his cloak. Jesus stopped in his tracks. "What's wrong?" the disciples must have asked themselves. "What's happening? What's the problem? We're wasting time!" "Who touched my clothes?" (Mark 5:30b NRSV), Jesus asked, maybe demanded, wheeling about and searching the crowd with his gaze, almost, it seemed, as if he were offended that someone in the jostling crowd had dared to brush his garment. "There's a whole crowd thronging about you," the disciples replied. "What do you mean, 'Who touched me?' What's the difference? Let's get on with the program." Jesus, Mark tells us, had immediately felt power go forth from him when the woman had touched his cloak—and at that very moment, she had been healed of her affliction. Scanning the crowd, after a few seconds or perhaps several minutes, Jesus saw a woman coming toward him, reluctantly, we may suppose, trembling with fear. She fell down before him—like *Jairus* had done—and she told him what she had done, and why. "He said to her, 'Daughter, your faith has made you well; go in peace, and be healed of your disease'" (5:34 NRSV).

Her disease had made her a social outcast and a religious pariah—she had had a flow of blood for twelve years, and had spent everything she had on doctors who had done nothing to help her, while her condition had grown steadily worse. Not the sort of thing she could talk about in public, though just the sort of thing that would set *others* talking about *her*, and something that made her ritually unclean under the law. She wasn't supposed to touch anybody, and nobody was supposed to touch her. But when she had heard that Jesus was in town—the man who was said to have power to heal difficult cases of sickness and disease—she ventured out to find him, and dared to reach out and break the religious taboo in hope that what she had heard was true. And it was! But now, she feared the consequences. Maybe he was a magician who would demand payment. Maybe he was a proud man who would insist that her impudence be punished. But when she made clear her need and her faith, she discovered that he was a man of love and compassion. "Daughter, your faith has made you well; go in peace, and be healed of your disease" (5:34 NRSV).

It wasn't just a matter of healing, of course. She was now in a position to be restored to community—to her friends and family, who had put her at a distance; to the normal routine of life, from which she had been distanced by the curse of her affliction. The Greek word for "heal" also means "save." And in the moment of her being cured by boldly acting upon her faith, she had also been saved from her isolation, saved from her embarrassment, saved from her despair.

Though Mark tells us the name of Jairus, the leader of the synagogue, the penniless and afflicted woman remains nameless. Probably, that's the way the crowd, and the disciples, regarded her—just another face, insignificant, common, a mere nuisance, really, as they and Jesus were on their way to more important appointments. But her story, her despair and her hope, made her *just* as important to the Son of God (notice that he called *her* "daughter") as if she were the daughter of a well-respected and well-known religious leader. And, in fact, in the time Jesus had taken, had spent, had "wasted" in the view of some, the daughter of the religious leader had died.

Mark shows us here that there is no hierarchy of need in the eyes of God—the problems of a beggar are just as important to God as the problems of a celebrity. In fact, rightly understood, desperation makes us *all* beggars before God, puts us *all* on the same footing with one another, makes us *all* brothers and sisters, equally the sons and daughters of God whose pleas tug equally on God's heartstrings. Almost anyone who has dealt lately with the health system in America can understand and sympathize with the woman's frustration. Anyone who has had a disease that would not go away, would not get better but only worse, can understand and sympathize with the woman's despair. But she ventured one more hope, based on the reports she had heard—reports that would undoubtedly have been ridiculed by the medical establishment and discounted by her HMO—and the faith that moved her to daring action resulted not only in her *cure*, but her *salvation*.

Anyone who has had a seriously sick child can understand and sympathize with the desperation of the synagogue leader. The possibility of a cure in such a case would bring parents to their knees. Dignity and pride of station become irrelevant. Wealth and prestige are suddenly pointless. There were probably some gasps in the crowd when the people saw who was coming toward Jesus, who was kneeling before Jesus, who was imploring Jesus to do what he had done for others—"Just lay your hands on her," Jairus begged, "and I know she will get well." Imagine such faith! Imagine being so tantalizingly near and then suddenly so impossibly far with the report, "Your daughter is dead. Why trouble the teacher any further?" (5:35b NRSV). Why had Jesus wasted precious time on that silly woman, who should be *punished*, not *rewarded*, for what she did? Surely, those who had overheard what had transpired had some such reaction. Jesus turned to the brokenhearted man. "Do not fear, only believe" (5:36b NRSV). Mark doesn't tell us the man's reaction to Jesus' words. He had hoped for a cure, because he had heard that Jesus could do such things. But death surely closed the door and set the lock on all hope.

The mourners were already on hand when Jesus arrived at the man's house—there was no question that the girl was really dead. The funeral had already begun. But Jesus chided them for weeping and wailing. "The child is not dead, but sleeping" (5:39b NRSV), he said. They laughed at him. They had seen her, some of them. They *knew* death, and they knew that no platitude or euphemism could change its reality. But the touch of *God* can—can bring life where there is none, like Michelangelo pictured the touch of God giving life to Adam in the fresco on the ceiling of the Sistine Chapel. "[Jesus went in and] took her by the hand and said to her, 'Talitha cum,' which means, 'Little girl, get up!' And immediately the girl got up and began to walk. . . . [H]e told them to give her something to eat" (5:41–42b, 43b NRSV). And Jesus next went to his hometown and taught in the synagogue, where people said, "Oh, it's just the son of the carpenter who lived down the street. Where did he get so high and mighty?" "And he could do no deed of power there," Mark reports, "except that he laid his hands on a few sick people and cured them. And he was amazed at their unbelief" (6:5–6 NRSV).

There are a lot of lessons in this passage—the lesson of faith ventured and faith rewarded, the lesson of God's power over not only disease, but even death, the lesson of human perception being much less than divine reality. But in the interweaving of the story of the desperate need of a social outcast and the story of the desperate need of a respected official, Mark is also offering us a lesson about the priorities of God. It is a lesson about those whom society considers to be expendable and those whom society considers to be important, and perhaps the way the *church* has too often looked at people, as well. It is about the Son of God being willing to be inconvenienced, delayed, and imposed upon by a woman who had nowhere else to turn, penniless, despised, rejected, alone, even though his appointment calendar was full with a real media event. It is about pastors taking the time to listen to their humblest parishioners, realizing that nothing in their job description is more important. It is about denominations supporting and not abandoning churches in the poorest parts of the inner city. It is about making room at the table, in trust that God's grace in Jesus Christ is adequate for all. It is about Christians in society insisting that their politicians not defame or disregard the poor and the needy and that presidents and kings and governors and legislators and judges exercise their responsibility under the testimony of scripture to do what is right and just and fair and compassionate. It is about recognizing that we are all beggars of God's grace—none of us entitled to it on account of our titles or our résumés, none of us *more* entitled to it than any *other*, *all* of us dependent upon the one who rewards our hope with wholeness. It is about God's priorities of salvation, in which no one's need is unimportant, in which no one's hope is disregarded, in which no one is overlooked or left out who reaches out in faith to touch even just the hem of Jesus' robe, trusting that his power is a sign of his love, and that his love is the prescription for every desperate need. And it is about the unspeakable joy of salvation and the miraculous gift of eternal life.

Fourteenth Sunday in Ordinary Time

First Presbyterian Church, Ponca City, Oklahoma
July 5, 2015

2 Samuel 5:1–5, 9–10
2 Corinthians 12:2–10
Mark 6:1–13

"Strength through Weakness"

OVER THE PAST SEVERAL years of increasing venom in our public discourse, paralleling notably the increase of airtime claimed by radio and television political talk shows, I have come to appreciate the *New York Times* columnist David Brooks. Though I am sure that he and I seldom vote the same way on election day, I find him much more intellectually honest than most commentators, whether conservative *or* liberal, and though I sometimes disagree with his conclusions, I very much respect his opinion and *his* respectfulness of *other* people's opinions and the difficulties involved in the decisions that our leaders have to make. So I was interested in getting a copy of his latest book, *The Road to Character*, when I heard it mentioned on NPR and PBS several weeks ago, and Linda ordered it for me as an early Father's Day present to have to read on the recent long flight to Spain with my daughter.

David Brooks's book is a collection of biographical reflections on the lives of several individuals who, in his estimation, exhibited character in a way that is much different from the standards of our modern American culture of self-centered materialism, hunger for praise and thirst for attention, celebration of the individual and neglect of the common welfare. One of the traits he identifies as instrumental in the building of character is the ability and willingness to recognize and acknowledge one's own weaknesses and to commit serious effort to overcoming them.

He cites Dwight Eisenhower's temper and quickness to judge others, and how the general, then president, developed personal strategies to keep his temper in check and his thoughts about others under control, serving his superiors in the military, some of whom he detested as egotistical and petty, in a way that contributed to *their* effectiveness, and threading a moderate course through competing truths and amidst the sudden and dramatic lurches of postwar society. "Ike was even more divided than most of us," Brooks writes.

> He was a master of army expletives, but he almost never cursed in front of women. He would turn away if someone told a dirty joke. He was reprimanded at West Point for habitually smoking cigarettes in the halls, and by the end of the war he was a four-pack-a-day smoker. But one day he quit cold turkey: "I simply gave myself an order." "Freedom," he would later say in his 1957 State of the Union address, "has been defined as the opportunity for self-discipline."[1]

A lot of people these days either never admit a flaw or weakness, even to themselves, but come up with excuses for their own behavior that they would quickly judge to be wrong in others, or they broadcast their flaw or weakness as if it were a virtuous strength, shamelessly, immodestly, defiant of anybody else's opinions, including *God's* if they *believe* in God. In this, they appear to be emulating the celebrities of our day, so many of whom crave publicity no matter the reason, and whom the public throws dollars at, seemingly in proportion to the degree of outrage of what they say and what they do.

In today's epistle reading, Paul the apostle tackles the matter of personal weakness, which is sometimes interchangeable with the word "sin." Paul was not a perfect man, not even after his conversion from passionate persecutor of Christians to passionate follower of Christ while traveling to Damascus one day on a mission of hatred. Paul was not a perfect man, not even after he had had a vision and revelation of Christ that had lifted him up out of himself to the highest heaven. Paul was not a perfect man, not even after he had endured much suffering for the sake of the gospel and had also been successful in establishing churches throughout Asia Minor and Greece. And we mustn't suppose that the words of Paul were always welcomed by congregations that called themselves "Christian" any more than his words had always been welcomed in the Jewish synagogues and the public square. At Corinth, it seems, he had many opponents and rivals, preaching competing versions of the gospel and claiming special insight from God. Paul had

---

1. Brooks, *Road to Character*, 60–61.

always had to defend himself against the charge that, unlike other apostles, he had not known Jesus before the crucifixion, and there remained among many new followers of Christ a suspicion about this man who one day had been hauling believers before tribunals and had watched approvingly as Stephen was stoned to death, and the next day was saying that the risen Lord Jesus had appeared to him along the highway and made a believer out of *him*, which eventually led to his *own* being cursed and assaulted and jailed for the sake of the gospel.

There are enough references to his Jewish heritage and Roman citizenship that glint through his claims of *humility* to realize that Paul must have had a long and constant battle with pride. There is enough feistiness in his debates over his mission to the Gentiles that glints through his words about *submission* to realize that Paul must have had a long and constant battle with churchly discipline. It cannot have been easy for him to master control over those personality traits that might have constituted an obstacle to his apostleship and his modeling of Christ for his audiences and for the congregations that he started and continued to visit and hold in prayer and keep in correspondence. And it must have been irksome, indeed, to have what he described as a thorn in the flesh, or, more correctly in the Greek, a thorn "for" the flesh—some persistent annoyance, we don't know exactly what, of which he was constantly mindful.

It might be that his rivals in Corinth had been boasting of *their* ecstatic experiences, visions and revelations, implying that Paul's authority was inferior, that Paul's spirituality was weak. So he responded, in Second Corinthians, by saying that he knew a person "in Christ" who many years earlier had had an experience of rapture so enthralling that he didn't even know whether it was a bodily experience or a purely spiritual one. In order to avoid appearing to boast like his opponents were doing, Paul did not say that it was he *himself* who had had this experience, but as the passage continues, he undoubtedly was referring to his own faith awakening. Apparently, what he described was far more exceptional than what even his boastful rivals had claimed. It seems that he had kept it to himself for fourteen years, and even now, since the details of the experience had no bearing on building up the church, he wouldn't repeat what he had heard during his vision or revelation—things that were not to be disclosed to *anyone*.

We could speculate all day about Paul's ecstatic experience and the things that he heard, but there would be no use in doing that. And it would divert attention away from the point that Paul was really trying to make here. Wonderful as that experience was, beneficial as it might have been in asserting his authority and besting his opponents if he so desired, he explained: "Therefore, to keep me from being *too* elated, a thorn was given me in the flesh [or *for* the flesh], a messenger of Satan to torment me, to *keep* me from being too elated" (2 Cor 12:7b NRSV).

A lot of people have spent a lot of time over the centuries speculating what this "thorn" in or for the flesh might have been—a speech impediment, a medical condition, Paul's own personality—but that too is pointless, and it diverts attention away from the testimony that Paul was really making here. "Three times I appealed to the Lord about this, that it would leave me, but he said to me, 'My grace is sufficient for you, for power is made perfect in weakness'" (12:8–9a NRSV). Paul had learned that his weakness, his affliction—his sin, even, if it be that—had been used by "the Lord" to teach the apostle something that he otherwise would not have understood: he needed to rely on God, whose undeserved gifts are all that Paul required and exactly what Paul really needed, and *power*, strength for the task, is to be found in *weakness*—the experience of one's outward fate being in the hands of others, the knowledge that one's own abilities and intellect are not adequate to the job that needs to be done. Whatever Paul might have *preached* about relying upon God, whatever his *rhetoric* about humility might have been *in public*, he never really trusted in God enough to *depend* upon God *completely* until he was confronted with a handicapping disability that he could not make go away. And when he *prayed* for it to be *removed*, God did not answer the prayer the way Paul *wanted* it answered, but, rather, forced him to confront it honestly and grow beyond it, trusting not his *own* abilities to achieve perfection, but *God's*.

I myself think it very likely that this "thorn," this equivalent of a sharp tormenting stake, this constant annoyance, which Paul traced to Satan, was his own pride, and the resulting temptation to boastfulness that he found so un-Christlike in his opponents who were praising their experiences and abilities as if they were a mark of their own worthiness and superiority. Unlike *them*, *Paul* concluded, "I will boast all the more gladly of my *weaknesses*, so that the power of Christ may dwell in me" (12:9b NRSV).

If we think, deep down, that our strengths make us in any way self-sufficient, or that our achievements are a sign of our worthiness—which is a real temptation when we think we are really good at something, and even more so when we ignore our flaws and our failures—God has no way of entering our lives to shape our spirits, or, in David Brooks's vocabulary, to form our character. When you look back over the stories in the Old Testament, it was *not* when great people were at the top of their game that they were conscious of their need for God, or that God was able to use them as agents in the work of salvation. Moses was a fugitive living on the lam, timid and stammering. Jacob was running away from his justifiably angry brother, his mischief-making finally turning back on him. Joseph, arrogant and rude, was thrown into a pit and hauled off to Egypt. And David's astounding successes eventually blinded him to his own immoralities.

And, in the New Testament, Paul. Paul had to be disciplined by a prickling reminder, a rock in his shoe, so to speak, of his imperfection and dependence upon God and reliance upon a strength that was nothing he had or ever *could* achieve on *his own*, but came only through the crucified and risen Christ—the one whose *wounds* were the only way to *our healing*, the one whose *death* made possible the *only true life*, the one without whose *crucifixion* there could be no *resurrection*. "Therefore," Paul concluded his testimony about both his ecstatic experience and his debilitating annoyance, "I am content with weaknesses, insults, hardships, persecutions, and calamities for the sake of Christ; for whenever I am weak, then I am strong" (12:10 NRSV). Whenever he found himself in need, Paul was admitting, *that* is when God was able to infuse him with the source of *true* strength, reliance upon the same powerful trust in God's redeeming and merciful and sustaining love that shines through the cross of Jesus Christ. And so, indeed, he *did* endure weaknesses, insults, hardships, persecutions, and calamities for the sake of Christ—some inflicted upon him from *outside* the church, some inflicted upon him from *within*.

Have you prayed for patience and found yourself in positions where your patience was tried all the more? Have you prayed for the ability to love and found yourself confronted by someone whom it was very hard to love indeed? Have you prayed for understanding and found the world becoming more complicated by the minute? The response that *Paul* got to such prayers was just what *you* have experienced, and with that came the divinely bestowed awareness that God develops within *us* patience, love, and understanding by *putting us* in those *exact* places where patience, love, and understanding are *required*, forcing us to *confront* our weakness, our need, our sin, even, and *opening* ourselves to God, who *alone* can match our deficiency with grace and form us to Christlikeness.

The power of God that finds the opportunity to give strength when we recognize that we are weak—the power of God that raised Jesus Christ to eternal life when his enemies had put him to death—is the power of God that uses our awareness of our own *in*ability to make of us agents of God's salvation. Now, *that's* something to *boast* about.

Fifteenth Sunday in Ordinary Time

Spanish Springs Presbyterian Church, Sparks, Nevada
July 6, 2003

2 Samuel 6:1–5, 12b–19
Ephesians 1:3–14
Mark 6:14–29

"Predestined for Glory"

ONCE UPON A TIME, in sixteenth-century Switzerland, the French theologian John Calvin wrote some words about God's choice of people, God's election of people—words that Calvin considered to be profoundly comforting to believers at a time when the medieval Catholic Church was teaching that people had to do specific things, repent in specific ways, in order to be saved from the eternal fires of hell. God has already determined our destiny, long before we were even born, Calvin assured the believers; do not be anxious about your salvation. Then John Calvin wrote some more words about the subject, and then he wrote some more, and then he wrote still *more*, and pretty soon the very people he thought should find the message profoundly *comforting* were profoundly *terrified* that before they were even born, before the world ever came into existence, in fact, God had selected *some* people to be *saved* and *some* people to be *damned*, and Presbyterians have wrestled ever since with the task of defining "predestination" and trying to explain how a God of justice and love could do such a thing.

To be fair to John Calvin, he didn't *invent* the doctrine of predestination—he just wrote too much about it. In fact, he had simply rediscovered the theology of *Augustine*, the great fourth-century theologian from North Africa, considered one of the fathers of the early church. And to be fair to *Augustine, he* didn't invent the doctrine of predestination—he just gave it a name. In fact, he was only repeating what *Paul* had said in *his* letters in the New Testament. And to be fair to *Paul*, first Augustine, and then John Calvin, made it a much louder issue than the *apostle* did, and expanded it in ways that Paul never considered. John Calvin especially, and generations of Calvinistic theologians *after* him, including the people who wrote the Westminster Confession, rather logically pontificated that if God had chosen *some* people for *salvation* from before the world was created, then God must have chosen *other* people for *damnation* from before the world was created. And a lot of Calvin's followers rather naturally concluded that if our destiny for heaven or hell is already decided before we're even *born*, then nothing we do or don't do in life, and whether we have faith or we don't have faith, really makes any difference; or rather, we have no choice with regard to faith and salvation, since the choice was already made long before we were even around. Now *that's* terrifying.

The only problem is, Paul didn't *say* that, and there is plenty of evidence, in scripture and in experience, that the wise purpose of God does not travel along the shiny rails of human logic. Didn't God work salvation by allowing his own Son to be killed at the hands of petty and jealous politicians and nervous and tradition-bound committees? That's hardly logical by human standards. "God chose what is *foolish* in the world to *shame* the *wise*," Paul testified; "God chose what is *weak* in the world to *shame* the *strong*" (1 Cor 1:27 NRSV). God does not choose as *we* would choose; God's wisdom extends much farther than our poor reasoning, especially when it comes to matters of salvation. On this point, the father of the Reformed faith and the spiritual forebear of us Presbyterians is guilty of fixing his attention far too keenly on *one* part of the Bible and neglecting the *gospel*—except that what he taught isn't even actually *in* the Bible, not even in *Romans*, where he rooted his doctrine of predestination.

In one of our Sunday morning adult classes, we have been looking carefully at Romans and noticing that when we examine the full scope of Paul's argument there against the backdrop of the situation in the Roman church that Paul was addressing, he was demanding that Christians, people who have faith in *God* and acknowledge the crucified and risen Jesus Christ as *Lord*, have an obligation to be tolerant of people with opinions that are far different from theirs—in fact, not only tolerant, but welcoming. Paul took it for granted that anyone in the church already *has* a relationship with God that is based on *faith*—faith that has come at *God's* initiative. Therefore, no one has any ground for questioning or criticizing or condemning the content or quality or expression of that faith.

Certainly, no one has any right to impose the particulars of his or her own faith on another person. One very practical reason for tolerance is that no one of us has the whole truth on our own, and if we think we have it bottled up in a single passage of scripture, we are denigrating the *rest* of scripture, and have violated the Second Commandment by making an image of God in the words of our creed. We need the *fullness* of scripture to be able to understand even a *part* of scripture. And if we open ourselves to the scriptures in their fullness, we will give God permission to surprise us, tease us, challenge us, humble us. For instance, when it comes to the subject of predestination, we need not only the testimony of Romans: "For those whom [God] foreknew he also predestined to be conformed to the image of his Son, in order that he might be the firstborn within a large family. And those whom he predestined he also called; and those whom he called he also justified; and those whom he justified he also glorified" (Rom 8:29–30 NRSV). We also certainly need the testimony of Ephesians:

> He destined us for adoption as his children through Jesus Christ, according to the good pleasure of his will, to the praise of his glorious grace that he freely bestowed on us in the Beloved. ... In Christ we have also obtained an inheritance, having been destined according to the purpose of him who accomplishes all things according to his counsel and will, so that we, who were the first to set our hope on Christ, might live for the praise of his glory (Eph 1:5–6, 11–12 NRSV).

The popular understanding of predestination is something that is more likely to produce despair than hope, to terrorize than to comfort, to make us arrogant than to make us humble, to lead to pride of self than praise of God. The "Left Behind" series of books is quite popular, and several people have told me that they are good. But we need to make sure that we do not succumb to any "nya-nya-nya-nya-nya" attitude about thinking of oneself as being among the chosen few. To put it bluntly, if the sheep and the goats are going to be separated in that way, how does the popular author know that the "rapture"—a word that can't be found anywhere in the Bible, by the way—didn't occur before he was even born? Or even one day while he was busy meeting with his publisher?

Maybe part of the problem is that we, like John Calvin, tend to fix our attention too much on the notion of predestination, and too little on the purpose or goal for which God has chosen us. Listen carefully to what Ephesians says: "Blessed be the God and father of our Lord Jesus Christ, who has blessed us in Christ with every spiritual blessing in the heavenly places, *just as he chose us in Christ before the foundation of the world to be holy and blameless before him in love*" (1:3–4 NRSV). God has chosen *us* to be what God created *all* people to be—"*holy*," set apart for God's own use, and "*blameless*," giving no cause to be accused or condemned. As God created *all* things to be in communion with him, as God called "good" *everything* that God created, so it was God's choice that *we* should be. In that, we are no different from any of the rest of God's creation. "He destined us for adoption as his children through Jesus Christ, according to the good pleasure of his will, to the praise of his glorious grace that he freely bestowed on us in the Beloved" (1:5–6 NRSV). The writer of Ephesians says this to his whole audience, not just to *some* of them. The destiny of being God's adopted children is shared by the whole community of faith, not just a few, and not just as scattered or random individuals. "In him we have redemption through his blood"—meaning his death on the cross—"the forgiveness of our trespasses, according to the riches of his grace that he lavished on us. With all wisdom and insight he has made known to us the mystery of his will, according to his good pleasure that he set forth in Christ, as a plan for the fullness of time, to gather up all things in him, things in heaven and things on earth" (1:7–10 NRSV).

God's plan isn't that some be *saved* and some be *damned*. God's plan is that, in time, *all* of creation will be *united* in *Christ*, the things that are in heaven and the things that are on earth, those who have died and those who are still living. Anything *less* than that would be contrary to God's will, and, ultimately, God's will must prevail. "In Christ we have also obtained an inheritance, having been *destined* according to the purpose of him who accomplishes all things according to his counsel and will, so that we, who were the first to set our hope on Christ, might live for the praise of his glory" (1:11–12 NRSV). Here, I think, is where we need to give our primary attention. We have been chosen, elected, destined, to live for the praise of God's glory. And here, surely, the Calvinists who wrote the first question and answer of the Westminster Shorter Catechism got it right: "What is the chief end of man?" "Man's chief end is to glorify God, and to enjoy him forever." We exist, we were brought into being, for the purpose of giving praise to God for God's glory—"to glorify God"—and to live in communion with God for all eternity—"to enjoy him forever."

The Bible declares that we are predestined to glory—but it is not *our* glory that is our destiny. It is *God's* glory. We have been chosen—clearly all of us in the church, and it *sounds* like all humankind—to live for the praise of God's glory, not to glory in others' praise of *us*. So our job isn't to speculate about one another's chosenness. Our job is to do those things that give praise to God for God's mighty acts of creation, for God's mighty acts of providence, for God's mighty acts of salvation, especially for the sacrificial death of his own Son Jesus Christ on the cross and for the miracle of raising his own Son Jesus Christ from the dead and seating his own Son Jesus Christ in power and authority in "the heavenlies," as the Greek wording of Ephesians says. "Predestination" is not about our privileged status, either on earth or in heaven. Ephesians testifies that predestination is about the purpose for which you and I and everyone else was brought into being—to praise God's glory. And all the rest of scripture testifies that praising God isn't just a matter of singing songs and waving hands; it's a matter of living and behaving and serving in ways that *please* God and promote God's *purpose* and respond to God's generous *love* and abundant *mercy* by being generous with *our* love and abundant with *our* mercy. And, indeed, in the very next paragraph, the writer of Ephesians commends his readers and gives thanks for the love that they have shown.

You and I have been chosen by God. But that is not an exclusive privilege. In fact, it is neither "exclusive" nor a "privilege," in the popular sense of the word. You and I have no way of knowing, and so we should not even speculate about, the boundaries of God's elect. Knowing how God has been merciful to *us*, we are fully justified in having good hope that God will be merciful to *all* people—merciful beyond human understanding or even imagining. And our being "elect" in no way makes us superior; predestination gives no basis for *imposing* our understanding of God upon others, and it gives us no authority to cast *judgments* upon others. It *is a privilege*—the privilege of contributing to the eternal purpose that God, in wisdom and love, laid down before the foundations of the world. But it is a privilege realized in serving others humbly and selflessly, remembering the humble and selfless way in which Jesus ministered to all who had need, and remembering the humble and selfless way that Jesus died for even the most egregious sinner, and for you, and for me.

Openness, inclusiveness, tolerance—these things are not simply *options* for a church; they are not a matter of philosophy, or expediency, or outreach strategy. These things are rooted in faith in God as God has revealed himself in Jesus Christ. And when they are rooted in *faith*, not just a matter of philosophy or expediency or outreach strategy, and not simply selected from among many options but in fact part and parcel of who we are as people of faith, responding to our calling to give praise to God's glory, then openness and inclusiveness and tolerance express a rock-solid trust in God, not an uncertainty about God; then they testify to strength of commitment, not to weakness of conviction; then they give witness to the *only* way by which we may be saved, not to the shoulder-shrugging attitude that any belief is just as true as any other. And it will be clear, to anyone who cares to notice, that we have been "marked with the seal of the promised Holy Spirit" (1:13b NRSV), which is "the pledge of our inheritance toward redemption as God's own people, to the praise of his glory" (1:14 NRSV)—the very thing for which we were predestined.

Sixteenth Sunday in Ordinary Time

Spanish Springs Presbyterian Church, Sparks, Nevada
July 20, 2003

2 Samuel 7:1–14a
Ephesians 2:11–22
Mark 6:30–34, 53–56

"And the Walls Came Tumbling Down"

THE JERUSALEM OF JESUS' day was a large, cosmopolitan city. Once upon a time, virtually everybody in the city would have been Jewish. But in the first century, Palestine was a Roman province, and so there were Roman soldiers in Jerusalem. There were merchants and other people of commerce who would have come to the city from other nations on business, some who even lived there—commercial agents and ambassadors and so on. Various people might have drifted in from the rural regions neighboring Israel, as people have always been attracted to cities for the prospect of work or excitement or whatever. It was a large, bustling place, and some of the people doing the bustling would have been Gentiles.

Some of the Gentiles would have become interested in the Jewish religion, and, from time to time, would have come to the temple precinct. Some of the Gentiles would simply have been impressed by the magnificence of Herod's temple, and come to see it as tourists are attracted to large, ornate buildings the world over. Gentiles were permitted inside the outer wall of the temple complex, in what was known as the "Court of the Gentiles," but not within the temple itself. That was reserved for Jews, and the presence of a Gentile there would have defiled the sacred place where God was thought to make his earthly address. Even Jews who were considered unclean under the law for some reason could not enter the temple itself until they had been ritually cleansed, but Gentiles *never* could.

The walls of the temple were physical representations of the barrier that the law constituted between Jews and Gentiles—a dividing line quite as imposing and impenetrable as the stone bulwarks of the temple. Those who adhered to the laws and regulations of the covenant could enter into the privileged company of God's people. Those who were uncircumcised and did not regulate their lives by the intricacies of the law were excluded. But in Jesus Christ God changed all that. When Christ died on the cross, the walls came tumbling down, the New Testament testifies, and even the uncircumcised, even those who failed to regulate their diet according to the prescriptions and proscriptions of the law, even those who did not, perhaps *could* not, participate in the various Jewish feasts and festivals, were now at no disadvantage as far as God was concerned. "[N]ow in Christ Jesus," says the writer of Ephesians, "you who once were far off"—meaning the Gentiles, the non-Jews—

> have been brought near by the blood of Christ. For he is our peace; in his flesh he has made both groups into one and has broken down the dividing wall, that is, the hostility between us. He has abolished the law with its commandments and ordinances, that he might create in himself one new humanity in place of the two, thus making peace, and might reconcile both groups to God in one body through the cross, thus putting to death that hostility through it. (Eph 2:13–16 NRSV)

The ultimate purpose of God, Ephesians testifies, is to bring the whole created universe into an all-embracing unity in Christ. That unity is foreshadowed and indeed actually begun in the church, where a divided humanity is brought together, as even Jew and Gentile are united in a single community of faith and worship, of life and love. It isn't that differences are *wiped out*, but that the *rationale* for the distance is *removed*. The *law* is no longer the way that anyone is saved, but the sacrificial death of *Christ*, so Gentiles are no longer disabled or disadvantaged by not being followers of the Jewish law. It isn't that the law was never any good, according to Ephesians, but that the law has now been overcome by the death of Christ, and, with it, the impediments to unity between Jew and Gentile. What God has purposed from the beginning for all people has now begun in the church. "So then you are no longer strangers and aliens," Ephesians says of the Gentiles who have responded to the Christian gospel, "but you are citizens with the saints and also members of the household of God, built upon the foundation of the apostles and prophets, with Christ Jesus himself as the cornerstone. In him the whole structure is joined together and grows into a holy temple in the Lord; in whom you also are built together spiritually into a dwelling place for God" (2:19–22 NRSV).

By the time Ephesians was written, Herod's temple had been destroyed, as had much of Jerusalem, when the Romans quelled the Jewish uprising in the year 70. But the true temple of God still existed, Ephesians asserted: it is the church—not a building, but a people; not a place bejeweled with emeralds and rubies and glinting with gold and silver, but a people ornamented with kindness and mercy and shining with love and unity. Ephesians calls Christians "members of the household of God" and a "holy temple in the Lord." *This* temple was in the process of being built up as believers of Jewish and Gentile background prayed together, ate together, worked together, gave praise together. Unlike the temples of Solomon and Zerubbabel and Herod, *this* temple had a foundation built not on lifeless stones but on the witness of martyrs, of apostles and prophets, and this temple had a cornerstone not of granite or marble but of the flesh and blood of Jesus Christ.

There had always, in Israel, been a tension between the freedom of God and the desire to build a dwelling-place for God. In the Sinai, God might have been frustrated by the people's grumbling unfaith and the people might have been frustrated by their errant wandering and lack of grocery stores, but it was an experience in which, in the long run, God's dependable faithfulness was demonstrated and a relationship of trust was built. God was present among the people as a pillar of cloud by day and a pillar of fire by night and in the tent of meeting when they stopped to rest. Once they entered the Promised Land, once they extracted God's begrudging approval to have a king, once the threat of the Philistines was overcome, David decided to build himself a palace of fine cedar wood, and then, embarrassed by the grandeur of his own home and the humbleness of God's tent, David proposed to build God a temple. But God responded through the prophet Nathan that God did not want, God had not asked for, God would be offended at the notion that he could be confined, tamed, domesticated in a house made by human hands.

It has always been unclear how what was so objectionable during *David's* reign was suddenly acceptable and unopposed during *Solomon's* reign—he *did* build a temple for God in Jerusalem—but the whole episode reveals the uneasiness that comes with the notion of God being assigned to a place, to a building, to anything that looks like God is at our beck and call, that God is only relevant certain hours of certain days, that God is under control. And that danger didn't end with Kings David and Solomon. It may well be that when the word "church" came to be applied to a building with a steeple on top, rather than a group of people with the Spirit of Christ in their midst, it became easier to suppose that what people do *outside* the church building isn't much God's business, that politics isn't God's concern, that the other six days of the week are a time when God's commands to care for the poor are subordinate to market economics, and God's will for harmony and reconciliation is subordinate to nationalism and war-making, and God's claims upon our resources are subordinate to our tastes for leisure and power and stocking up for a future in which God may prove undependable. I can testify from recent personal experience that concern about a building can come to dominate the agenda of a congregation and very definitely its pastor, no matter how hard you try to keep it in the perspective of being only a tool for worship and education and mission and service.

The cities of the Roman Empire were filled with temples, and as the emperors declared themselves to be gods, the citizenry of this place and that vied with each other to win the emperor's favor by building temples for the imperial cult. There was, of course, only one temple for the God of the Hebrews, the God of Jesus Christ, the only true God in all the universe, and when the Roman army destroyed it, it was never rebuilt. Ephesians calls Christians "members of the household of God" and the "holy temple of the Lord." Once, in a dispute with the leaders of the Jews in the temple, Jesus had said, "Destroy this temple, and in three days I will raise it up" (John 2:19 NRSV). The Jewish leaders—including, perhaps, even some of the temple priests—assumed that he was talking about the building they were standing in, and they found Jesus' saying ridiculously absurd. But of course he was talking about his own body, as scripture says, and his disciples remembered, after the resurrection, what he had said.

Ephesians metaphorically speaks of the church as being *like* a building—a holy temple—but at the same point makes it clear that the church is not *really* a building, but the people whom Christ has united, both Jew and non-Jew. The dividing wall has been broken down. The law with its commandments and ordinances has been abolished, and can no longer separate peoples into camps of "holy" and "unholy," "clean" and "unclean," "circumcised" and "uncircumcised." It happened on the cross. Now Jesus is the cornerstone, or the Greek word might be translated "capstone" or "keystone"—the architectural element that holds everything in place and is paramount to the whole structure. There is no distinction now—and all people can see that God's plan from the beginning has been a "new creation" that requires abandoning the barriers that once distinguished Jew from Gentile. They are members of a household held together by one capstone, Jesus Christ, who fits together and holds in place all the diverse materials in a spiritual building that no fire or earthquake or invading army can destroy. The walls have come tumbling down, and, paradoxically, the true temple has been erected. God is not confined in any place, either in Jerusalem or in Sparks, Nevada. Access to God is not restricted to the holy few, flashing their credentials of righteousness at the entrance gate, but is present in villages and farms and marketplaces and wherever people have need—even just by touching the fringe of Jesus' cloak. Where Jesus is, God is. Where Jesus is healing, God is working salvation. Where Jesus is forgiving, God is tumbling out mercy. Where Jesus is showing compassion, God is revealing love.

Where is Jesus now? Not shut up in a building made of stone and wood, but at the head of a living, breathing, flesh-and-blood locus of God's saving activity in the world—the church, not a place but a people, not a matter of geography but a matter of love, not a cold edifice but a living body. It is a temple in which the walls that divided the common from the holy, one person from another, human beings from God, have all come tumbling down. It is the spiritual structure in which God's eternal purpose of unity is being realized, and enmity and hostility between God and creation and between individuals and between communities and between nations are overcome, because, in the sacrificial death of Christ, there is no longer room for pride or envy or jealousy or greed. "In [Christ Jesus]," Ephesians testifies, "the whole structure is joined together and grows into a holy temple in the Lord, in whom you also are built together spiritually into a dwelling place for God" (2:21–22 NRSV). Not a building, thanks be to God, but a people; not walls of separation but a Spirit of unity; not the tyranny of the law but the gracious love of Jesus Christ. And so this door is open to all.

Seventeenth Sunday in Ordinary Time

First Presbyterian Church, Dodge City, Kansas
July 24, 1994

2 Samuel 11:1–15
Ephesians 3:14–21
John 6:1–21

"Fish, Loaves, and Faith"

"Mama!" the boy shouted as he ran into the house. "Mama! Guess what, Mama!"

"Not so loud. Slow down. Why all the fuss?" said the bedraggled woman as she looked up from her household chores, pushing a stray curl up under the scarf on her head. "You'll wake the baby!"

Indeed, there came from the back room the soft sound of rustling bunting, behind a curtain drawn across a doorway.

"But Mama," the boy came over to her and started tugging at her skirt, "it was wonderful. And it wouldn't have happened without me. He said so!"

The woman stopped what she was doing and stood straight up from her bent-over position. Her hand instinctively returned to her forehead to replace the habitually unruly curl, but this time it had remained in place under the scarf, so instead she just wiped her brow with the back of her hand. She was a woman perhaps in her mid-twenties, but prematurely middle-aged, as so many wives and mothers were in this working-class village near the Sea of Galilee. Keeping house was difficult enough in those times. But the Passover celebration was only a few days away, and the housework had increased with the anticipation of family and friends visiting. She had not even had time to go to market that day, and so had sent her young son to buy some fish and bread for supper.

He was a typical boy, affectionate and surprisingly warm-hearted at times, dependable enough when there were no distractions, but scarcely conscious today of the extra burden placed upon the woman of the house by the approaching holiday. Just now, he looked up at her with big, bright eyes, and a smile which could barely contain the report of some great adventure. "Mama!" he said again. But just at that moment, she noticed that he was empty-handed.

"Where are the fish and bread that I sent you to get? And where is the basket that I gave you?" Her knitted eyebrows betrayed a vexed attitude. "Didn't you go to the market? I have too much work to do here today. Surely you could do this one thing for me that I asked you to do."

"Yes, Mama, I did just what you said. I got the fish and the bread. But let me tell you—"

"Then where are they? That was to be our dinner tonight."

"He took them, Mama. He used my fish and my bread."

"What are you talking about? Did someone steal them from you?"

"Oh no, Mama. I offered them to him."

"What, to a beggar? We will be beggars too if you give all of our food away."

"Mama, please listen. He's not a beggar, and he didn't steal anything from me. He needed it to feed the people. He said he couldn't have done it without me offering him my fish and my bread."

"*Our* fish and *our* bread," his mother corrected him. She had grown impatient, as adults do. "Where are they? Tell me what has happened!"

"I'm trying to, Mama. I went to the market, just like you told me. I bought two fish and five loaves of bread—the brown kind. And I was bringing them back home. But as I was coming from the market, there were a whole bunch of people walking up from the dock."

"O Lord, what shall I do with such a child?" the woman rolled her eyes upward. She closed them a few seconds in exasperation, and then looked back down at her son, sternly now. "There is work to do here to make ready for Passover, and I need your help, not to have you run off with the—"

"But Mama, I thought it must be important—so many people! There must have been a jillion! Anyway, they just went out on the hillside. It wasn't so very far. But let me tell you what happened."

"Just tell me where our dinner is," she answered dryly.

"Well, I heard some of them saying how hungry the people were, so I—" The boy began to sense that his mother shared none of his excitement, and he was beginning to doubt now whether she would understand the mood of generosity that had come over him and prompted him to give away their supper. "I gave them to this man."

"What man?"

"Well, he seemed to be in charge of things."

"And what did this man who seemed to be in charge of things do with *our* fish and *our* bread?"

"He used them to feed all the crowd."

"And how did he feed 'a jillion' people with two fish and five loaves of bread, eh?"

"Well, he did. He just . . . did!" The story was sounding a little implausible even to the boy now; as he remembered what had happened, it defied even his boyish logic. Why had he ever thought that his mother would share his enthusiasm? He looked up at her, the face that he knew so well that he sometimes forgot that he loved it, the dress that he knew so well that he never thought about why he had never seen her wearing any other one. "He really did," the boy muttered.

The look of bewildered disappointment in her son's down-turned face—that he had done something that *he* thought was right and proper and could not fully comprehend why *she* thought that it was foolish and wasteful—now touched the woman's heart, and she put her arms around the boy and drew him close in her embrace. "We just don't have money to throw away like that," she said gently, hoping that he would somehow understand why she was upset. "Times are hard right now," she explained, thinking to herself that times are *always* hard.

"But Mama, they were hungry!" he pleaded, and he started to cry, burying his face in her dress. "I thought—"

The woman sighed deeply, her son's tears moving her to sorrow that she had scolded him. And she even felt a little pride in her son, somehow. "It's all right. We'll manage." She knew, of course, that they *would* somehow get along. They always did.

She released her embrace when she heard a loud banging on the door of the house. "Oh no, they'll wake the baby!" she said, half to her son and half to herself. The boy darted toward the door and opened it.

"Have you heard what happened? Have you heard about the miracle?" It was the woman who lived down the street, a typical village busybody, but today animated by some bit of news beyond any previous level of excitement. "Oh, but of course you have," she said, now noticing for the first time the boy standing in front of her, his hand still on the door handle. Remaining in the doorway, the visitor looked back into the interior of the room at the boy's mother. "It was a miracle! It was a miracle—no doubt about it! And I was there to see it—just imagine! And the bread and the fish were *real* too; I ate some! And this dear boy of yours"—she had never spoken of him that way; in fact, she had always seemed to find much that was objectionable about any children but her own—"this dear boy of yours had a part in it all. What a good little boy. You really must come to see this man who fed all these people. I'm on my way now to find my husband to take him back out to hear the man speak." She turned and bustled toward the next house, where she pounded on the door just as loudly or more so. From the back room, mother and son could hear the baby working up to a cry, but they just looked at each other, the mother with an expression of confusion, the boy with an expression of vindication, his hand still resting on the handle of the open door.

Suddenly, the room was shadowed by the figure of a large, muscular man standing just outside the doorway. He was looking down at the boy. "They told me where you live. You forgot this," said the man to the startled lad, and the man handed him the market basket he had taken with him earlier that day. But his mother could detect from her position in the middle of the room that the basket was now obviously far from empty, for her son strained when the man handed it to him.

She walked toward the open doorway with a questioning look. The man was a Galilean, she knew from his speech, and his dress suggested that he was one of the fisherfolk.

In the dim light, the stranger had not noticed her at first, but now that she moved toward the door and put her hand on her son's shoulder, he acknowledged her presence with a smile. "I just met your son a little while ago," he explained. "He's a fine boy—and a generous one. You must be proud."

She nodded, still with a questioning look on her face, and somewhat embarrassed to be addressed by a man whom she did not know.

Suddenly, the man recognized the awkwardness of the situation. "I'm sorry, I should not have startled you. My name is Andrew. I live in Capernaum, across the lake. My people are from Bethsaida. I am traveling now with Jesus, the Nazarene. Your son did us an invaluable service today. But"—he looked back down at the boy with a kind expression—"he forgot his basket."

That drew her mind back to the basket and the burden that it seemed to contain. She glanced down and was amazed at what she saw—it was filled with morsels of bread and fish enough to last her family for days! She looked back at the Galilean fisherman, her mouth open in amazement.

"I must go now, back to Jesus and the others," he said to the mother and son. "Thank you again for your generosity," he concluded, looking down now at the boy and tousling the lad's hair with his big calloused hand. Then he turned back into the street.

The woman just stared at the fish and the bread.

"It's like I told you, Mama. And the other man—the one who was in charge—said that it was my fish and bread that made it all possible."

The woman did not go out to join the crowd, as her neighbor had urged; there was still the Passover to prepare for. But over the next few days, she heard more reports of the miraculous feeding of the crowd, and how, indeed, it had all started with her son's offer of the fish and bread that he carried in his market basket. She heard other reports, too, concerning the man about whom her son had spoken, this man Jesus—strange stories about his walking across the waves to join his companions in their boat, about how he had healed many people of their diseases and infirmities, about how he referred to himself as "bread"—the bread of life. She thought about all these things. But mostly, she thought about how she had *chided* her generous, kind-hearted boy for offering their own little supper to Jesus so that "a jillion" hungry people might have something to eat.

Eighteenth Sunday in Ordinary Time

First Presbyterian Church, Dodge City, Kansas
August 3, 1997

2 Samuel 11:26—12:13a
Ephesians 4:1–16
John 6:24–35

"Growing Up Together"

JUST A FEW YEARS ago, a very popular book declared that all we really need to know, we learned in kindergarten. The chapter that gave Robert Fulghum's book its title talked about things like sharing everything, playing fair, not hitting people, putting things back where we found them, cleaning up our own mess, saying we're sorry when we've hurt somebody, taking a nap every afternoon (I would *really* like to try that one), and, when we go out into the world, watching out for traffic and holding hands and sticking together.[1] Reverend Fulghum says that if we just applied the basics that we learned in *kindergarten*, even the world's biggest problems might well be solved.

It is a clever premise, and of course it's true, so far as it addresses how to get along with other people and take care of ourselves and our planet. But there is also a level at which, even if these simple lessons of kindergarten were learned well, we *still* need to learn *more* to survive in our imperfect world, downhill from Eden. If we literally *stopped* with a kindergarten education, with knowing how to use crayons and paste and scissors and counting up to one hundred and learning the letters of the alphabet, who would raise our crops? Who would build our houses? Who would cure our diseases? Perhaps the better message is *not* that we should *stop* with what a kindergartner knows, but that we should never *forget* what *we learned* in kindergarten. For in a world of complex natural forces and

---

1. Fulghum, *All I Really Need to Know I Learned in Kindergarten*.

strong emotions and the constant fact of sin, we *do* need to learn more than kindergarten provides.

Families and society at large cannot survive on the basis of what six-year-olds know and feel and yearn for. The presence of children in our midst is a precious gift and a great joy—their innocence, their energy, their honesty, their simple justice. But if the world were nothing but a population with the appetites and capacities and whims of little children, it would be no paradise, but a mess. Childish behavior is *appropriate* to *children*. It is *not* appropriate for *adults* to behave childishly, as they sometimes do, especially when they do not get their way in a group. Wisdom born of experience has led most societies to require *more* than a kindergarten education. We may well lament the loss of innocence and energy and honesty and simple justice that seems to happen with more advanced learning. But we know that growing beyond childish ways is *important* if we are to cope with *adult* cares and *adult* responsibilities.

I don't know of any minister who would recommend a book titled *All I Really Need to Know About Faith I Learned in Sixth-Grade Sunday School*. Yet, a lot of Christians—church members, even—seldom discuss the faith with others, never take part in religious education after sixth grade or so, which means, when you think about it, that there are a lot of adults trying to operate in an adult world, with adult temptations and adult powers and adult problems, on the basis of a child's understanding of God. Important as worship is—and it's *imperative* for anyone who takes God's holiness seriously—worship isn't the same thing as religious education. A sermon, if it's really a sermon, isn't a lesson plan. Reading the Bible or devotional literature alone and privately isn't a substitute for Christian fellowship and studying with other Christians—we need the companionship and insights and experiences of other people of faith to keep us from drawing individualistic, self-serving, and even bizarre conclusions about the gospel, and supposing that Christianity is only a particular set of *beliefs* and not a distinctive way of *living*. Some adults think that trying to operate with a faith understanding that is appropriate to a *child* is a *virtue*. Biblical literacy is at its lowest point in modern history. Is it because a lot of people who claim to believe in God have somehow decided that the less they know about the Bible, the better off they are? "Reading the Bible only confuses me," one woman told me in a former parish. And the very word "theology" is regarded by a lot of people these days with suspicion and even ridicule—suspicion and ridicule fostered, in part, by certain voices within the church itself.

Jesus commended child*like*ness when he talked about our entering into the kingdom of God. But Jesus *never* suggested that child*ish*ness is a virtue. And the Pharisees and the scribes and the chief priests and, occasionally, the disciples themselves were so childish in thinking and deciding and speaking and acting on the basis of an immature faith that they missed *entirely* the significance of Jesus standing in their midst. Take, for instance, the episode in today's Gospel reading. The people had just fed on loaves and fish miraculously multiplied by Jesus, and yet they still demanded of Jesus a "sign" that he was sent from God, that they might believe in him. "Do not work for the food that perishes," said Jesus—*Do not think only of your stomachs, as* children *might do*—"but [work] for the food that endures for eternal life" (John 6:27a NRSV). Jesus saw that all this crowd was *really* interested in was a free meal, when these people *should* have recognized their hunger for *Christ himself*, the Savior. They thought of God as the heavenly Santa Claus satisfying their wish for candy. Jesus was offering them the very bread of life—life's only *real* meaning, life's only *real* solace, life's only *real* joy. They had the kindergarten-type God down pretty well. But they weren't in kindergarten anymore. They were in the *adult* world of sickness and death and injustice and tyranny and famine and oppression and sexuality and war. They needed an adult faith. They needed to come to the unity of faith and of the knowledge of the Son of God. They needed to grow into the measure of the full stature of Christ.

When faith does not continue to develop beyond a childhood level, how can it support us in adult trials, comfort us in adult sorrows, offer hope in adult need? If faith is arrested by our failure to continue learning, failure to continue questioning, failure to continue opening oneself to the Holy Spirit's work of confronting and testing and stretching, failure to be in conversation about the faith with other Christians, then how are we to grow beyond childhood? A *simple* faith is a *treasure*, but a *simplistic* faith is a *waste*. Every tremor will seem to us to threaten the very foundations of our home life, of our life as a congregation, of our life as a denomination. Every doubt will seem as dangerous as planting a foot in hell. Every disappointment will pose a crisis of damning proportions. Every headline will spark anxiety. And if we are left to ourselves to manage *alone* in the world with a *childish* faith, God's purpose of redeeming creation will not be fulfilled in us.

Augustine, the most important Christian thinker since Paul, had a hard time growing up. Some of you may know the story of his immaturities. He flitted from one philosophy to another, from one religion to another, chasing whatever appealed at the moment. He was ruled by his lusts for so long, he was so promiscuous, and yet his mother, Monica, continued to pray for her son to settle down with God. Some of you know that Augustine was not only a great theologian, but a great champion of the monastic life—not the hermit sort of existence that idealized isolation, but life in a community of believers, disciplined, mutually supportive, praying for one another. In his famous book titled simply *Confessions*, Augustine remarked of his early adulthood that as he grew *older*, he never really grew *up*. Long beyond childhood, he kept playing the same games over and over—deceptions, thefts, conquests. His games had slightly different objects as he came to adulthood, but they were still the same old games, with the same old rules and the same old aims and the same old marks of failure or success, but no longer excusable as the innocence of childhood. He had wasted so much of his life running after this satisfaction or that, but he found no satisfaction until he found Christ, or, rather, until he allowed Christ to govern his desires and control his tempers. He attributed his finally maturing in faith and in life much to the example and the prayers of his churchgoing mother, and he came to value highly the influence of *other* believers as he grew up into Christ. The community of faith—the fellowship of the Christian congregation, the brotherhood of the Christian monastery—Augustine knew and esteemed. The church, he recognized as a gift of God.

Do you think of the church as God's gift to you? I have mentioned before the misfortune that the English language does not distinguish between the singular and the plural second person, as Greek does. The English word "you" can refer to a single human being or to a multitude of people. The individualistic experience of life on the frontier, and perhaps the individualistic emphasis of capitalism, have combined with the individualistic responsibilities of Puritanism to answer for one's own sins, to read the scriptures as if every "you" were direct to each of us as so many individuals. But in Greek, the word "you" in the New Testament is usually plural. The Bible was written to be read in *groups* of people—in congregations, where people sit side by side in worship with the folks they work with and go to school with and eat with and argue with, and know that it all applies to all of them in their life together. To be a Christian means not just to *believe*, but, equally important, to be and function as an integral and necessary part of the whole body in unity—not in uniformity, not without diversity, but yet each part knitted securely into one community, each member making a unique and vital contribution to the whole. The Bible is the church's book, written *for* the church; baptism and the Lord's Supper are the church's sacraments, gifts for the building up and maintenance of the whole body. We do not just read the Bible in isolation. We do not baptize in private. We do not receive the bread and the cup in solitude. They are not just about the salvation of the individual, but about the life of the community of the faithful. So with the appointments of the Spirit. "The gifts [the risen Christ] gave," says Ephesians,

> were that some would be apostles, some prophets, some evangelists, some pastors and teachers, to equip the saints for the work of ministry, *for building up the body of Christ*, until *all of us* come to the *unity of the faith* and of the *knowledge of the Son of God*, to

> *maturity*, to the measure of the full stature of Christ. We must *no longer* be *children*, tossed to and fro and blown about by every wind of doctrine, by people's trickery, by their craftiness in deceitful scheming. But speaking the truth in love, *we must grow up in every way* into him who is the head, into Christ, from whom *the whole body*, joined and knit together by every ligament with which it is equipped, as each part is working properly, promotes the *body's* growth in *building itself up in love*. (Eph 4:11–16 NRSV)

"I believe the Bible, pastor, I believe whatever the Bible says, and I read it and pray about it too, but I'm just not into coming to church—not into all that worship falderal, not into Sunday school, not into church dinners, but that's my church, all right, I'm on the rolls there." Do we believe what the Bible says about *growing up together*? Look around. Look around in the sanctuary. Look around in the church school classroom. Look around in the fellowship hall. Look around at mission sites. Scripture says, and experience shows, that we must grow up in every way into him who is the head, into Christ; a *childish* faith isn't a proper faith for an *adult*. And we can only do that, scripture says—we can only grow up in our faith—within the context of the body of Christ—in the company of believers, worshiping together, praying together, sharing together, studying together, serving together, rejoicing together, weeping together, enjoying God's precious gift of the church together. Here should be our dearest relationships, the family into which Christ has adopted us, the believers whom we have pledged to support in times of need and *with* whom we have pledged to celebrate in times of joy and to *bear* with at *all* times. The church exists for the purpose that we may *grow up* in faith, and we can only grow up in *faith* if we grow up *together*. Egotism and individualism and self-indulgence destroy unity and wreck community. The task of growing from childhood to adulthood is to overcome egotism and individualism and self-indulgence and set them aside as we understand that we have responsibilities *to* and responsibilities *for* something larger and more complete than ourselves. Growing in faith means acknowledging responsibilities to Jesus Christ, the bread of life, and responsibilities for the community of faith for which Christ died, and which he continues to nourish through his flesh and blood—the church.

"All I really need to know I learned in kindergarten." Well, not really. But it would be good not to forget the things that we *did* learn in kindergarten—among them, to share, and to watch out for traffic and hold hands and stick together. And, if we want a mature faith, a faith that is in the measure of the full stature of Christ, a faith that *matters*, then we must not forget what we surely learned in Sunday school even as children—the importance of *continuing* to grow up *together*.

Nineteenth Sunday in Ordinary Time

First Presbyterian Church, Ponca City, Oklahoma
August 9, 2015

2 Samuel 18:5–9, 15, 31–33
Ephesians 4:25—5:2
John 6:35, 41–51

"Rogues to Riches"

FOR THE PAST SEVERAL Sundays, the lectionary has guided us to Ephesians for our epistle reading. All of the New Testament epistles have to do with the church, one way or the other. But the letter to the Ephesians has often been called "the church's epistle." No other part of the Bible presents in such a lofty manner Christ's hope for his church—not just for *individual* believers, but for the *church*. The Gospels—Matthew, Mark, Luke, and John—hint at what church life was like at the time of the evangelists; when *they* wrote about Jesus, they were reflecting on what Christ meant for their own congregations, established years after the crucifixion and resurrection. In the letters of Paul, we listen in on part of a conversation between the apostle and certain congregations he knew that were experiencing trials and difficulties of various sorts. But Ephesians was not a letter occasioned by any particular problem; in spite of its title, Ephesians might not even have been sent to any particular congregation. Not having any specific congregational crisis in mind, or any theological debate to address, the writer of Ephesians—probably a protégé of Paul—was free to write in broader terms about what the church is called to be and to do.

In the passage from Ephesians that we read for today's epistle reading, there is a lot of general teaching about being truthful, about being careful what we say, about being kind—all of which is absolutely necessary in *any* church deserving of the name. At first glance, the letter could pass as that middle-of-the-road, go-to-church-now-and-then-because-it's-the-thing-to-do type of religion practiced by middle-of-the-road, go-to-church-now-and-then-because-it's-the-thing-to-do Christians. But nestled in the middle of this general and rather bland moral encouragement is a sentence that seems sort of amazing to be addressed to a group of churchgoers: "Thieves must give up stealing" (Eph 4:28a NRSV). The writer of this great letter about God's intention for the church and for our life together as Christians felt compelled to include a commandment against stealing. Why? Can you imagine your pastor looking into this congregation some Sunday morning and saying, "You thieves out there, you're going to have to give up your stealing"? What would you think? Has the pastor gone out of his or her mind?

Probably, not one of us supposes that there has been a genuine thief among us since First Presbyterian Church was organized more than a century ago. We think, somehow, that they don't belong among good, decent Christian folk. We would not really expect to *attract* thieves, and can't imagine them sitting *among* us. Does Ephesians mean to suggest that some congregation or congregations in the first century of Christianity actually had *thieves* in them? Well, apparently so. All *sorts* of people were being attracted to the gospel in those days. All *sorts* of people were being awakened to faith by the power of the Holy Spirit, hearing and learning and responding to the good news of Jesus Christ, discovering in him the very bread of life, the nourishment without which no one can truly live. All *sorts* of people were finding a home in the church, finding a *family* in the company of believers, finding a welcome at Christ's table. *Some* of them, apparently, were even genuine *thieves* who had to be told in the clearest of terms not to steal anymore. *Some* of them, apparently, were not nice, kind, well-mannered, gentle people, but bullies—hard, wrathful, profane, and slanderous. *Some* of them, apparently, were not who you would expect sitting next to you in the pew of the average Presbyterian church. *Some* of them were out-and-out rogues.

Ephesians reminds us that the gospel *isn't* something for the respectable, pious, solid citizens of the kingdom of the *earth*, but for abject sinners, otherwise hopeless, who yearn to be citizens of the kingdom of *heaven*. Can you picture the scene, can you imagine the impact, of the world's riffraff sitting and perhaps squirming in their seats, some of whom might have come originally to jeer and ridicule, but who found themselves touched and transformed by the words, "Put away from you all bitterness and wrath and anger and wrangling and slander, together with all malice, and be kind to one another, tenderhearted, forgiving one another, as God in Christ has forgiven you. Therefore be imitators of God . . . and live in love" (4:31—5:2a NRSV)?

Until this passage popped up in the lectionary for today, I had always read over too quickly that part about thieves giving up stealing. I had never considered what a remarkable glimpse that is into the life and practice of the early church. I think that most of us tend to picture those early Christians as mainly simple, good-hearted people, somewhat uncomfortable with the ways of the world, grieved by its evils, alien to its lusts, well on their way to a greeting-card salvation when Jesus happened to come along at the right time and lift them just a little bit higher so that they could get up over the threshold of heaven. The Barabbases weren't interested in following Jesus, and the Judas Iscariots quickly fell away, leaving only the gentle, the meek, the basically good—you know, people like us, or like we *think* we are. And then we read Ephesians, this high-water mark in thinking about the church, its glorious mission and its blessed riches of salvation, and we are face to face with the *astounding* fact that the pedigree of the body of Christ includes liars, slanderers, blasphemers, and thieves. A single sentence confronts us not only with the profound *change* that the gospel requires in people, but also the radical *acceptance* that the church is supposed to extend. Yesterday's rogue is today's imitator of God! Yesterday's thief has a claim upon the riches of heaven!

Most of us consider ourselves respectable folk. In spite of our unison prayers of confession, our sin remains theoretical for a lot of us. Many of us probably think that we are really somewhat *worthy* of salvation, especially when we compare *our* faults with *other* people's faults. It probably wasn't with thieves and other such rascals in mind that *this* church was founded over a century ago. I'm sure that it was regarded more as a place where the respectable folk of Ponca City could associate with other respectable folk of Ponca City to do what respectable folks are *supposed* to do. We're talking about the *church*, after all—the bride of Christ, pure and spotless. But, holy as the church is, respectability and an impeccable résumé and keeping the right company are *not* the ticket that admits people to a Christian church, according to scripture; rather, entry into Christ's church requires an acknowledgment of need, a recognition of failure, a blemished past, and a contrite heart. It isn't the person who is *sinless* who has the promise of eternal life, but the person who *believes*. It isn't necessarily the church of the *upper crust* that wins Christ's approval, but the church that welcomes the hungriest *sinner*, and freely offers the bread of *life*. We who steal by way of collecting stock dividends from companies that muscle smaller companies out of the market, we who steal by way of purchasing products manufactured in low-wage sweatshops, we who steal by way of taking away someone's good name with a careless comment, perhaps we don't understand the radical break with the ways of the world that Christ requires. The thieves addressed in Ephesians understood it. Perhaps *we* can't understand salvation as well, or value grace as highly. Perhaps it's more difficult for us really to understand Christ's intention for his church.

Not many people come into the Presbyterian Church as new believers. We need to ponder that fact. One of the characteristics that mark the mainline churches and most, but not all, of their congregations is that the majority of their members were either *born* into the church or *transferred* in from *another* mainline congregation. In general, we Presbyterians and our mainline friends do not do a very good job or reaching out to non-Christians. The established denominations have tended to forget that the very reason the church *exists* has to do with gracious invitation, being open, being welcoming, to anyone who senses their distance from God, their need to repent, their lack of saintly credentials. Membership statistics reflect that we're not very active in meaningful evangelism. The vital task of the church isn't the *maintenance* of the *righteous* so much as it is the *salvation* of the *unrighteous*, which comes about not so much by *condemning sin* as by *uplifting to holiness*, and it never means *changing* the gospel, but *living* it.

The realization that the person sitting next to us might have come through the church door with a long history of sin should not disgust us; it should cause us to rejoice! The purpose of the church is being fulfilled! The rogue has discovered where the riches are; the beggar has reached out for the bread of heaven! The church is being faithful to God's intention of welcoming lifelong sinners into the arena of salvation! And, when we stop to think about it, isn't that really *all* of us—lifelong sinners? And so there is hope not only for people with a history of stealing, but for people with a history of telling falsehoods, of speaking evil of others, of bitterness and wrath and anger and wrangling and slander and malice. Only, now we know we are to put all these things away, and to be kind to one another, tenderhearted, forgiving one another as God in Christ has forgiven us—and so be imitators of God, living in love as Christ loved us.

So never be scornful of *anyone* who approaches this table. It does not feed those who are *full*, but those who are *empty*. It is not for people who have *no need* of *salvation*, but for people who *acknowledge* their *sin*. It is not for folk who are self-sufficient, but for folk who are dependent upon the grace of God and the love of Christ. It is not for men and women who think that the riches of earth and heaven are theirs by right, but for men and women who are thankful for every undeserved blessing from the hand of God. It is for the church of sinners forgiven and accepted and loved. Just so, the riches of heaven are meant for the most desperate rogue—even for you, and for me.

Twentieth Sunday in Ordinary Time

First Presbyterian Church, Dodge City, Kansas
August 17, 1997

1 Kings 2:10–12; 3:3–14
Ephesians 5:15–20
Mark 6:51–58

"A King's Wisdom"

ASK ANYONE WHAT HE or she knows about King Henry VIII, and chances are that you will get the answer, "He had six wives." Ask anyone what he or she knows about King Midas, and chances are that you will get the answer, "Everything he touched turned to gold." Ask anyone what he or she knows about King Solomon, and chances are that you will get the answer, "He was wise." It's a common saying—"the wisdom of Solomon." There is the incident of the two women, each of whom claimed that a certain child was her own, and Solomon's decree that the little boy should be divided in two, knowing that the real mother would give up her claim rather than see her son killed. There is the attribution of the book of Proverbs to Solomon—that vast collection of maxims and adages that have proven to be so true over centuries of human experience, many of which have been chiseled into our memory.

In actual fact, Solomon was not *always* wise in what he did—he disobeyed God on several occasions, and God's anger at Solomon had serious consequences. But what most people know about Solomon was the great wisdom of which he was *capable* when he remembered to be faithful to God. And what could be more *important* in a ruler than *true wisdom*—a right understanding and proper discernment, being able to put oneself in another person's position and to view a situation from the true perspective.

Scripture tells us that Solomon genuinely loved the Lord, even to the point of building a great temple for him, with fine materials and richly appointed. Early in his reign—and Solomon was relatively young when his father David died and Solomon succeeded to the throne, perhaps around twenty years of age or so—the youthful king had a dream. He had gone to a place called Gibeon—a high hill, probably the site of an old Canaanite shrine, maybe a place where many people came in the hope of having a religious vision. The Lord appeared to Solomon in his dream, and asked Solomon what he, the Lord, should give him. Solomon answered that the Lord had been steadfast toward his father David, and now God had lifted Solomon up to David's throne, remembering the covenant he had made with David that *his* house should rule Israel. Solomon humbly acknowledged his own youth and inexperience, and the daunting task that lay ahead of him—ruling God's chosen people, such a great multitude. Invited freely to ask for *anything*, Solomon said, "Give your servant therefore an understanding mind to govern your people, able to discern between good and evil; for who can govern this your great people?" (1 Kgs 3:9 NRSV). He *might* have asked for a long life; like other people, kings want to live to old age, not only for their own sakes, but also for the sake of their subjects. He *might* have asked for military victories and the slaughter of his enemies; in an age of invasion and conquest, being a strong and effective ruler was commonly thought to mean battle and booty. All of these things a king might have been expected to request of God. But Solomon did not ask for these things commonly sought after. Instead, he asked for something much more precious, something that is much more difficult to achieve. "Give your servant an understanding mind," he said. "Give me wisdom." And

> [i]t pleased the Lord that Solomon had asked this. God said to him, "Because you have asked this, and have not asked for yourself long life or riches, or for the life of your enemies, but have asked for yourself understanding to discern what is right, I now do according to your word. Indeed I give you a wise and discerning mind; no one like you has been before you and no one like you shall arise after you. I give you also what you have *not* asked, both riches and honor all your life; no other king shall compare with you. If you will walk in my ways, keeping my statutes and my commandments, as your father David walked, then I will lengthen your life." (3:10–14 NRSV)

Scripture tells us approvingly about Solomon's humble petition for what a king should most desire—to be a wise and discerning servant of the people, a humble and faithful lover of God.

Compared with other kings we know, Solomon already *had* an *uncanny wisdom* when he *asked* for wisdom. Henry VIII kept asking for a *son*, and when he didn't *get* a son, he asked for a *divorce* so that he might marry some *other* woman who was foolish enough to *promise* him a son. Finally, he *did* have a son, Edward, who succeeded him but died in his teens, to be succeeded by Henry's daughter Mary, the bloody wrecker of the English church, and finally his daughter Elizabeth, one of the most successful of all monarchs, but not at all what Henry had hoped for. In retrospect, Henry lacked wisdom when it came to marriage, and even when it came to matters of succession. According to Greek legend, King Midas of Phrygia asked Dionysus, the god of wine, to grant him the power to turn to gold everything he touched. The god of wine complied with the greedy but unwise wish, and Midas was surprised to see his daughter turn to gold when he touched her, and his food even, so that he desperately begged Dionysus to take back his cursed gift. Better he had asked for wisdom.

Sometimes in history classes that I have taught, participants have expressed the frustration that the books always focus on the famous and the infamous, the decisions of governments and the battles of armies. Historians traditionally have not paid much attention to the things that mattered most to ordinary folk—what life was like for the average citizen, what was most important to parents and children, what concerned merchants and farmers and customers. History, including the historical books of the Bible, seems preoccupied with the powerful and the mighty, but most of us live among the average and the common. The affairs of state, the strategies of diplomacy, maps spread out in war rooms, seem far remote from the daily routine around the school desk and the workbench and the kitchen table. What is *our* interest in the dusty stories of an ancient king? None of *us* will ever have the opportunities *Solomon* had. None of *us* will ever have *his* responsibilities. What difference does it make to *us* that the Bible offers the case of Solomon as a yardstick for measuring the faithfulness of *all* kings? Is it simply so that we can hold up our prime ministers and presidents to God's standards and find them wanting?

I think that politics has probably always had its nasty side, though the nastiness seems to have gotten worse during my lifetime. Certainly the jokes about political figures have gotten raunchier, and some people speak without the slightest respect for some of our high officials or even their spouses. Personally, that's not how I was raised, and I find a lot of it contrary to the gospel by which I try to live. Christianity has always taught *respect* for properly constituted authority. Certainly the Reformers taught obedience to lawful rulers except in cases of the most extreme ungodliness. Jesus himself told his listeners to render unto Caesar the things that are his due. Some of the modern disrespect may be reaction to political boast and bravado. Humility is not a common trait in politics, certainly not in elective politics. Probably, not a single American president has ever been elected because he was self-effacing—not even Washington, not even Lincoln, not even Coolidge. It is said that Harry Truman quoted Solomon's prayer when President Roosevelt died and the man from Independence was thrust into the Oval Office following what was the nearest thing America has ever had to a kingly reign, both in terms of length and authority and public affection. But I'm not sure that humility is the trait that most people would associate with President Truman. Surely, no one can enter upon the presidency without praying, sooner or later, for wisdom. But *having* wisdom is not enough. In our era of instant polls and ruthless ridicule, a wise leader also needs the courage to *follow* that wisdom. Every Christian should pray regularly for our public officials to *have* and to *exercise wisdom*, and not only for our *own* leaders, but the leaders of *all* nations. I hope that is a routine part of your daily prayer.

Of course, the writers and the editors of Kings were not only interested in how *monarchs* behave. Their greater interest was in what God expects of his covenant people. Humility and obedience weren't just issues for the king, but for all of Israel, God's holy nation. The story of Solomon's request for wisdom, and his being wise enough to recognize his own human inadequacy for the task ahead, are told as a lesson for *all* of us. None of us is truly wise without God, and all *human* wisdom is *folly* compared with the wisdom of *God*. None of us chooses good over evil on our own. All of us should strive to be faithful and righteous and upright of heart, and recognize that if we succeed, it is not our own doing, but God's doing. And if the greatest person in the land is first of all a servant of others, as even *Christ* the most perfect king of *all* was a *servant* of *others*, then humble servanthood is the example *we* should follow. Riches and fame and power are not what the faithful person craves, nor the wise person, but the understanding from which flow faith and love and kindness and generosity and mercy and fairness and hope. And not just knowledge of facts and statistics and strategies and programs, not just information such as you can read in encyclopedias and briefs, but perceptive understanding—that prayerful knowledge of God's will that scripture calls "wisdom."

The Christian faith honors as the *highest wisdom* the very sorts of things that the *world* calls the *greatest folly*—giving one's possessions away for others and giving *oneself* up totally to God, forgiving those who abuse us over and over again and praying that they will be blessed, choosing death over disobedience—all of the things for which the cross stands. That is what the Christian faith identifies as wisdom. The Christian prays for such wisdom for her- or himself, and the courage to follow it above all of the things that the *world* calls wise—money, possessions, popularity, and the power that comes with them—all the things that are commonly associated with great rulers, the ones who have a secure place in all the history books. The *Christian* believes that the *poorest peasant* may be wiser than the *mightiest emperor*, and far *richer* too, though born in a *stable* instead of in a *palace*, though offering *himself* for the sustenance of *others* rather than taking what *others* have and adding it to *his own* wealth, though trusting God to provide his daily bread rather than wasting his days *hoarding* what God has promised to give *freely*, though sharing stories of *hope* rather than issuing compulsive *decrees*, though *inviting* to *discipleship* rather than *conscripting* to *soldiery*, though delighting in the simple joys of *fellowship* rather than manipulating others to personal *advantage*, though *surrendering* himself to an unjust *death* so that *others* might have *eternal life* rather than *clinging* to life for his own satisfaction. The Christian prays for the wisdom to conduct his or her life according to faith in Jesus Christ, the King of Kings, who said that even Solomon in all his glory was not arrayed as magnificently as the simple field lily, which neither toils nor spins, but lives and grows according to whatever comes from the hand of God (Luke 12:27 NRSV).

And Solomon prayed, "'And now, O LORD my God, you have made your servant king in place of my father David, although I am only a little child.... And your servant is in the midst of the people whom you have chosen, a great people, so numerous they cannot be numbered or counted. Give your servant therefore an understanding mind... able to discern between good and evil'" (1 Kgs 3:7a, b, 8–9b NRSV). "Pilate asked [Jesus], 'Are *you* the *king* of the Jews?'" (Mark 15:2a NRSV). Would you be like a king? Then pray for the *true* King's wisdom.

Twenty-first Sunday in Ordinary Time

First Presbyterian Church, Ponca City, Oklahoma
August 23, 2015

1 *Kings 8:1, 6, 10–11, 22–30, 41–43*
Ephesians 6:10–20
John 6:56–69

"Where We Meet the Infinite"

OF ALL THE DANGERS the Christian gospel faced in ancient times, the greatest threat was from a corruption of the Christian faith that historians call "Gnosticism." The word is coined from the Greek word *gnosis*, or "knowledge." More sinister than government persecution, more pernicious than the intrigues of priests and Pharisees and scribes, orthodox theologians quickly judged it to be a heresy. For it was a teaching, a belief, that only *particular* people are saved by God, who imparts to them a superior *knowledge*, a possession of facts and theories by those God deems to be specially *deserving*. According to the Gnostics, it was not in atonement for the unworthy that Jesus of Nazareth died on the cross.

Of all the dangers the Christian gospel faces in *modern* times, the greatest threat is from that *same* corruption of the Christian faith that historians call "Gnosticism." More sinister than communism, more pernicious than the rantings of Madelyn Murray O'Hare, it is *still* a heresy, fed and honed by the Enlightenment and finding manifestations in both mainline liberalism and right-wing fundamentalism, an assumption that our salvation is all about what we *know*, what we *think*, rather than what God has actually done in Jesus Christ and what *we* actually do in *response*. Depending upon the circumstances, it is used as an excuse for not worshiping with *other* believers on the Lord's Day and it is used as an excuse for not receiving communion *every* Lord's Day; it is used as an excuse for not calling government and industry prophetically to account and it is used as an excuse for not engaging in ministries of compassion and correction. There is an echo of Gnosticism in every utterance of that sophisticated objection "I don't have to be in a worship service to worship God," and in every sophisticated assertion that "I'm spiritual, just not religious," and in every sophisticated retort that "I believe in Jesus Christ but I don't want anything to do with his church."

A long time ago, in the days of King David and King Solomon, there was a debate within the nation of Israel about whether to build a temple, a place where people would gather to perform rites of remembrance and rituals of worship of the God who had brought their ancestors up out of slavery in Egypt and had accompanied them across the Sinai Desert. Much later, but still a long time ago, in the days of John the evangelist, there seems to have been a debate within Christianity about whether it was necessary to gather with other Christians to perform rites of remembrance and rituals of worship based on the words and actions of Jesus that highlighted his fleshliness, his incarnation. There were those in David's and Solomon's day who said that it was *wrong* to build a temple for God—that people would begin to think that God, the infinite, could be confined to a building made with human hands and bearing an earthly address. There were those in John's day who scoffed that the Lord's Supper was a crude ceremony that was *unnecessary* for anyone who knew all about Christ and was spiritually close to him. But the Bible rejected the claims of those who sought so to intellectualize God that a special place of worship was unimportant, and, later, those who sought so to spiritualize Christ that the Lord's Supper was nothing more than a memorial of the *Last* Supper, unnecessary for the believer, except perhaps as an occasional nod to Jesus' command when he was at dinner with his disciples, "Do this in remembrance of me" (1 Cor 11:24b NRSV), if even *that* were necessary.

No, the presence of God, the experience of God, cannot be limited to a building, no matter how fine its construction, no matter how pious its builders, no matter how precious the memories that are attached to it. And in too many instances in the past, both ancient and recent, people of faith have become so attached to a *building* that it has taken over their conception of the *church*. Indeed, they come to refer to the *building* as "the church" rather than the people who *worship* there—a use of the term "church" that surely would have appalled the apostles. Yes, a person can confess sins and give thanks to God and even hear God communicating on a golf course or on a ski slope or on a boat on a lake, perhaps even at the shopping mall or the ball field. And worship can and did take place in believers' homes.

But the very limitlessness of God, who is infinite and invisible and omnipresent, makes it all the more necessary for us to have *particular* places specially set aside for worship, if we are indeed to worship God with our whole heart and mind and soul, with daily cares and worldly associations and natural distractions at a minimum so that we may set our hearts and minds and souls on the heavenly and the eternal. And it is not just about the *place*—it is also about what we *do* there. Some ritual of affection is necessary to keep love alive between a people and their God, just as rituals of affection are necessary to keep love alive between spouses. As one commentator has phrased it, human beings need some trysting place with the infinite, just as, the Ten Commandments recognize, human beings need some appointed *day* of the *week* for a tryst with God. So Solomon the wise built the temple in Jerusalem not in order finally to provide a vagrant God with a *home*, but so that the *people* of God would have a place to come together to raise their voices united in prayer and hear together about their *common* destiny under God's providence. Neither *humankind* nor *God dwelt* in the temple, but there they would meet, and the very act of assembling together was an act of faithfulness by a people who were grateful and who were seeking to be obedient.

We are at the point in the life of this church that we need to consider options for how and where we will continue to meet God together for worship on the Lord's Day and other occasions, for church school and youth groups and adult education events, for fellowship meals, for planning of mission, for administration of our common life. And the place to *start* is to think together about what a church building is and what a church building symbolizes, itself containing and prominently displaying strong symbols of the historic faith—cross, font, table, pulpit with an open Bible on it.

Over the course of my ministry, I have become more and more impressed with another important symbol of our faith—one that we take for granted or easily overlook. I am aware and the session is aware that some people do not like being in the fellowship hall for worship this summer, where our seating has been more circular or around tables. Some people don't like sitting where they have to look at each other; personally, I never cared much to look at the backs of people's heads, sitting in rows as if we were in a classroom or at some amusement in a theatre. But I hope you will consider that our being in here this summer has helped us recover—at least for a few weeks—one of the primary symbols of the Christian faith that desperately needs to be reclaimed: the assembly of believers—not sitting all face-forward as if passively attending a lecture or an entertainment and essentially disconnected from each other, isolated even though in the same room, but *gathered*, physically and actively, around the Word and sacraments.

That's what the New Testament's word for "church"—*ekklesia*—means: "gathered." The very act of coming together to praise God, to confess our sins and ask for forgiveness, to listen for God's instruction and direction, to declare our faith, to give thanks and to pledge our commitment, all in public and in one another's company, is a profound act of faith—one might even say the *principal* act of faith. We *cannot* and *mustn't attempt* to domesticate the Creator of all things or try to box in the All-Powerful. But we need an appointed place and time to come together weekly and on other occasions to renew and confirm our relationship—a relationship that the Bible and all history testify is fundamentally communal and is necessarily forged and nurtured within the parameters of time and space.

We cannot touch an abstraction. But we *can* meet the Infinite, because the Infinite has deigned to encounter us within the world of sense and sight in human form—the person of Jesus, the Christ, whom the first disciples could see and hear and touch, and whom, when he broke bread and poured wine and said, "[M]y flesh is true food and my blood is true drink" (John 6:53 NRSV), they could, as it were, even smell and taste. Salvation is all about his offering up his body on the cross, pouring out his blood in a way that all the sacrifices of bulls and lambs and doves in the temple had never achieved, *could* never achieve. But those who accepted his invitation to dine with him in worship, to participate on *earth* by eating the bread and drinking of the cup as in the *heavenly* banquet at which the bread satisfies completely and the wine never runs out, were both participating in and giving testimony to the salvation that Christ worked on the cross, feeding on his teaching and drinking of his mercy just as if eating his life-giving body and drinking his life-giving blood. "[T]he one who *eats this bread* will live forever" (6:58b NRSV), Jesus said—not just whoever *knows* about me or whoever *thinks* about what I *taught*, not just whoever *remembers* the Last Supper or whoever *says* he or she *believes*.

It is uniquely and especially in gathering together, hearing the words of the book spoken and interpreted, eating and drinking at this table, that we are regularly able to meet the Infinite, to acknowledge that we are in the presence of the one who cannot be confined to any place, to touch and handle things unseen. And there is something important, profound, and very necessary for us who may *think* that we know all *about* it—all about God, all about Christ, all about the Bible, all about the sacraments, even—to actually *do* it, and to do it *in community with each other*, and to *declare* by our doing it that, even as *sophisticated* as we are, even as *intelligent* as we are, even as *spiritual* as we are, or maybe *because* of those things, we need a specific time and a designated place to gather together to sing, to pray, to listen, to vow, in one another's sight and in one another's hearing and in one another's touch, lest we come to assume that our salvation is really our *own* doing after all.

Like believers of old, we need always to be on guard lest we begin to assume that we have tamed God Almighty, lest we begin to suppose that we have pinned down God, who is bigger than the universe he created, lest we begin to imagine that Christ is magically sacrificed anew when we break bread and pour wine, lest we begin to think that the church is a building. But the hazard on the other side—supposing that faith is really just a matter of right thoughts, that God is aloof or unconcerned about events in the world, that worship is a matter of inconsequence at best or trendy preference at worst, that the sacrament is just an option for the believer, that we need no regular time and appointed place to come together to worship the God who entered history and geography in Jesus of Nazareth and continues present with his church in the power of the Holy Spirit, that salvation is a thing that is unconcerned with the stuff of flesh and blood and disconnected from the Son of God unjustly put to death on the cross—that is the *greater* danger of our age.

Take a look around this assembly. Take a look at each other, gathered together around the bold words and strong symbols of the Christian faith—the words of eternal life, the bread which, when eaten, sustains us to live forever. Here is where you and I and all of us together have the privilege of meeting the Infinite.

Twenty-Second Sunday in Ordinary Time

Spanish Springs Presbyterian Church, Sparks, Nevada
September 3, 2000

Song of Solomon 2:8–13
James 1:17–27
Mark 7:1–8, 14–15, 21–23

"When Cleanliness Is Next to Godlessness"

SOME TIME AGO, I stepped into a sandwich shop for lunch on what was clearly a bad day for the manager. It was just the manager and a young man behind the counter, with a long line of customers waiting to be served. By overhearing the manager's conversation with each customer ahead of me in turn, always including an apology, I learned that he was short on help that day, and that the young man working with him was brand new on the job. Behind the counter, confusion reigned. I probably should have gone somewhere else for lunch, but I had a craving for a meatball sandwich with mayonnaise, tomatoes, lettuce, green peppers, and grated Parmesan cheese, and I didn't know where else to go for one nearby. So I stayed in line.

Finally, after many minutes, I got to place my order, and I too received the now-rote apology from the manager. But my attention was really on a little drama unfolding between the young helper and the woman in line ahead of me. "Wait a minute," she was saying to the boy behind the counter. "Didn't you just make my sandwich without washing your hands after you handled the money from the person ahead of me?" "No, ma'am," the boy answered her, barely comprehending, I think, what she was asking. Well, in fact, I too thought that I had seen him go straight from the cash register to putting meat and cheese and lettuce and olives and pickles on the bread without visiting the sink. The woman rejected the sandwich and walked out of the shop. As I say, it was clearly a bad day for the manager.

The episode illustrates the great concern people have these days for hygiene, and understandably so, with reports of all sorts of bacterial horror stories in fast food restaurants and other places. Recently, though, television broadcasts and newspapers and magazines have been presenting medical opinions about how we may be overreacting. All of our antibacterial soaps and the like may in fact be *endangering* us by making us less resistant to common bugs, may even be denying our bodies the bacterial intake that is necessary to good health and proper digestion. At any rate, with our modern orientation toward scientific analysis and medical concerns, we may not quite understand what the real issue was that the Pharisees and scribes were raising one day about Jesus' followers not washing their hands before eating their meal. It wasn't an issue of hygiene, nor even one of social etiquette. In *their* tradition, at least, it was a matter of obeying God, and a matter of Jewish identity.

Specifically, the matter of washing one's hands before eating was part of the tradition that had developed *around* the law—what the Pharisees explained as the "fence" that kept the law from being violated and kept the Jewish people distinct from the pagans around them. For instance, the *law* says that you must not eat meat from a young goat that has been boiled in its mother's milk. The *tradition* of the scribes and the Pharisees was that you must never both eat meat and drink milk or eat any other dairy product at the same meal. For if you never both consumed a dairy product and ate meat at the same meal, you could not possibly violate, inadvertently, the actual commandment not to eat the flesh of a young goat that had been boiled in its own mother's milk. The Hebrew Bible nowhere says that you must wash your hands before eating. *Mom* might have said that, and *Dad* might have criticized you for coming to the table with dirty hands, but the *Bible* doesn't. Now, the market was a natural place to come into contact with foods and vessels and even *people* who were ritually unclean—Gentiles, or Jews who had been in contact with unclean things—and washing one's hands before eating what had come from the market was a way of purifying oneself from any possible contact with the unholy. But in a land of little water and no indoor plumbing, the handwashing requirement of the scribes and Pharisees was a burden, especially on the poor and the working class. In fact, *many* of the traditions of the scribes and the Pharisees posed a burden to the poor and the working class—something that God, through the prophets, prohibited as ungodly.

This may all strike us today as insignificant as the silly issue that caused six rebellions and thousands of deaths in Lilliput; *Gulliver's Travels* tells of the debate that had raged over several generations in that fictional land about whether to break an egg, before eating it, on the small end or on the large end. "Many hundred large volumes have been published upon this controversy," an informant explained to Gulliver, "but the books of the *Big-endians* have been long forbidden, and the whole party rendered incapable by law of holding employments."[1] So the author, Jonathan Swift, held up a mirror to the social pettiness of his time.

The question that the scribes and Pharisees asked of Jesus—"Why do your disciples not live according to the tradition of the elders, but eat with defiled hands?" (Mark 7:5b NRSV)—was, of course, a criticism not of the disciples, but of Jesus himself. The scribes and Pharisees were implying that if Jesus was not teaching his followers such rules of piety, then surely he could not be a religious teacher. Surely he was not interested in keeping the law. But in fact, based on his sayings that are reported in scripture, Jesus never advised *anyone* to violate or ignore the law of God as it was laid down in the Old Testament. In fact, Jesus frequently *expanded* the *literal* wording of the law to make it more encompassing. He taught, for instance, that divorce violates God's intentions for marriage, even though the law of Moses explicitly *permits* divorce under certain circumstances. The "tradition of the elders," as Mark called the business about handwashing, and washing food bought from the market, and cleansing cups and pots and kettles and other things that we today would think is only simple prudence, was nevertheless a *human* regulation, not a requirement of God's law.

What Jesus *did* object to was the way in which formalities—human inventions that *masquerade* as righteousness—come to preoccupy people so that they totally neglect the *purposes* of God that the *law* was meant to *teach*. The details of cleanliness upon which the scribes and Pharisees were so focused was taking the place, for them, of the purposes of God, and was certainly leaving no place for the *grace* of God. So Jesus responded to his critics that the sorts of defilement that violate the will of God are not *external* matters—whether one washes one's hands before eating, for instance, since what we eat just passes through the body anyway—but what comes from the heart. It's not what we put *into* our mouth that is the real issue, but the harmful things that can come *out* of it. It's not what we *touch* with our hands, but whether our hands are closed to those who are in need, and whether they are clenched into fists of hatred. The law deals specifically with what we *do*. But God is interested in what we *do* because it is an indicator of what we *think*—whether our loyalties and our beliefs, our outlook

---

1. Swift, *Gulliver's Travels*, 48 (emphasis added).

and our hopes, are faithful to God's purposes, to God's intentions, to God's expectations.

"Do you not see that whatever goes into a person from outside *cannot* defile . . . ?" (7:18b NRSV), Jesus said. "It is what comes *out* of a person that *defiles*. For it is from *within*, from the human heart, that evil intentions come" (7:20–21a NRSV). And he went on to list specific *acts*—fornication, theft, murder, adultery. But, ranking right up there with such *behaviors*, Jesus catalogued an even longer list of *attitudes* and *thoughts*—avarice, wickedness, deceit, licentiousness, envy, slander, pride, folly. "All these evil things come from *within*," observed Jesus, "and *they* defile a person" (7:23 NRSV).

In last week's Gospel reading, we read that many of Jesus' followers, when they heard him say that he was the bread that came down from heaven and that whoever eats this bread will live forever, were offended and complained and turned away from him. Jesus asked the twelve whether they also wished to go away, but Simon Peter answered, "Lord, to whom can we go? You have the words of eternal life" (John 6:68 NRSV). The epistle and Gospel readings today point to the fact that just *hearing* the words, though, is not enough. We must *do* the words. Coming to worship, seeking out Christ, is not the end of the process. In fact, it can be rather narcissistic, ego-boosting. We have to allow the Holy Spirit to implant the words within us, so that they can take root and flourish and shape us into the image of God, form us into disciples of Jesus Christ. External *formalities* are not the issue—the issue is the condition of the heart. And the condition of the heart is manifested by how we treat others—how we speak, how we behave.

As your pastor, I am almost embarrassed to preach to you people about the subject—most of you in this room are well aware of the facts that Jesus declared to the scribes and the Pharisees and to his disciples that day. You know well the truth of the letter of James: "If any think they are religious, and do not bridle their tongues but deceive their hearts, their religion is worthless. Religion that is pure and undefiled before God, the Father, is this: to care for orphans and widows in their distress, and to keep oneself unstained by the world" (Jas 1:26–27 NRSV). You know it. You practice it. But the fact of the matter is that we, nearly all of us, at some time or another have had some experience with church folk who did *not* bridle their tongue, who were *not* quick to listen and slow to speak and slow to anger, who considered their religion *not* a commission to be meek and humble but an invitation to bully and criticize. The meanest people I have ever known were among those who came nearly every week to the place where the words of eternal life were spoken, but who apparently never really *heard* the words, and so they did not *do* the words. A person can be a renowned philanthropist, the organizer of every charitable this and that, have never been sexually immoral or stolen money or killed anyone, and yet be greedy, deceitful (market analysts might call them "shrewd"), slanderous, full of pride and empty of genuine compassion toward the people around them. "All *these* things come from *within*," explained Jesus, "and *they* defile a person" (Mark 7:23 NRSV). "If any are *hearers* of the word and not *doers*, they are like those who look at themselves in a mirror," wrote James, referring to the situation of some Christians in the church that he knew; "for they look at themselves and, on going away, immediately forget what they were like" (Jas 1:23–24 NRSV). They wear the badge "Christian," they frequent the place where the word is spoken and check off each of the commandments, but after hearing what God demands, they go off and think and speak and behave in godless ways.

Perhaps you have been on the receiving end of the deceit or the slander or the folly—which means misplaced values—of someone who *obeys* the *law* and *ignores* the *gospel*. All the more incentive for you to be not simply a *hearer* of the word, but a *doer* of the word. We can murder a man or a woman in a hundred ways without actually killing that person. The Reformers reminded us that the Sixth Commandment means that we are required to *do* our neighbor *good*, and to *treat* our neighbor *well*. "Therefore rid yourselves of all sordidness" is a command not just to wash our hands before eating, but to let the word of God and the teachings of Christ scrub our hearts clean of all envy, of all jealousy, of all greed, of all judgmentalism, of all pride. Otherwise, we simply *can't* be *doers* of the word.

"[I]f any are hearers of the word and not doers, they are like those who look at themselves in a mirror . . . and, on going away, immediately forget what they [look] like" (1:23–24 NRSV). Go ahead and look in a mirror each day—not just to primp and coif but to see what the image of God looks like, and what a disciple of Jesus Christ looks like. But when you turn away from the mirror, don't forget who you are—a person cleansed for godliness by the waters of baptism and sanctified by the blood of God's perfect sacrifice so that you may be a *doer* of the word that the Holy Spirit is implanting in you. And if you *are* a *doer* of the word, everything you *touch* will become *holy*, and everyone you *meet* will be *blessed*.

Twenty-Third Sunday in Ordinary Time

Spanish Springs Presbyterian Church, Sparks, Nevada
September 6, 2009

Proverbs 22:1–2, 8–9, 22–23
James 2:1–17
Mark 7:24–37

"It All Begins Here"

OF ALL THE PASSAGES in the Bible, our Gospel reading this morning is one of the most difficult for people to understand. We think to ourselves, "These are not the words of the Jesus *we* know." The report that Jesus rejected a woman who came to beg him to cast a demon out of her little girl, and insulted her on top of that, hardly fits the picture that most of us have of the Savior. Some commentators have tried to soften the harshness of the scene by suggesting that Jesus was merely testing the woman's faith—presumably, testing her worthiness to have her innocent little child healed. But since when would the Son of a just and loving God make the *daughter's cure* dependent upon the *mother's faith*? Some have explained that the Greek word for "dog" here referred specifically to a household pet. But the fact is that, whether this word for "dog" meant a Pekingese or a pit bull, when it was applied to *people* it was degrading and demeaning, and it was *especially* so on the lips of someone who was ordinarily so careful to honor human dignity. A woman who was not a Jew—a Syrian woman living along the Phoenician coast to the north and west of Galilee—heard that Jesus was in town and sought him out and fell down at his feet and begged him to heal her little girl, and Jesus' reply explicitly drew attention to the fact that she was not a daughter of Abraham, not a Jew, and it seems clear that he would have let the child *remain* afflicted on that account alone, were it not for the dogged persistence and quick wit of the woman. "'Let the children be fed first,' said Jesus, meaning the children of Abraham, "'for it is not fair to take the children's food and throw it to the dogs.' But she answered him, 'Sir, even the dogs under the table eat the children's crumbs'" (Mark 7:27-28 NRSV). Perhaps the best thing that can be said about Jesus in this episode was that he was smart enough to know when he had been outwitted. "Then he said to her, 'For saying that, you may go—the demon has left your daughter'" (7:29 NRSV).

I will not pretend to you that I don't find Jesus' first response to the woman to be puzzling. In fact, I think it is appalling, it is so un-Christlike, and I can't explain it away. But I think that the reason this episode appears in Mark at *all* has very *little* to do with the healing itself and a *great deal* to do with Jesus' ultimate act of ministry for a foreigner in need, for someone beyond the pale of normal concern for a Jew. Look back just four verses in Mark, and we see that Jesus had just declared all foods to be clean—he said that it isn't what a person *eats* that defiles the individual, but what the person *says* and *does*. Whether a person eats a kosher diet or not isn't the point, Jesus said. That means that being a Jew or a non-Jew isn't the point, being a member of the house of Israel or being a Gentile isn't the point. And the very next episode in Mark finds Jesus being approached by one of those very people—a non-Jew, unclean by religious standards, not entitled to salvation under the law—with faith that Jesus has the power to heal her child, has the authority to cast out demons, has the almightiness of God—everything that the Pharisees and scribes and chief priests of the Jews denied and rejected. *Even a crumb, Lord, just a crumb, will be enough—a word and a gesture, and I know my child will be healed.* "So [the woman] went home, found the child lying on the bed, and the demon gone" (7:30 NRSV). And then Mark tells us that Jesus went on to another Gentile territory, and there he healed a man who was deaf and had a speech impediment, presumably another Gentile. There could not be a greater contrast to the proper, law-abiding religious types who remained deaf to Jesus' teachings and could not bring themselves to utter the praise that was due his name.

The true miracle here is not an exorcism and a healing. The true miracle is the overcoming of prejudice and borders. The power of God in Jesus Christ is available to heal whoever is sick, Jew or Gentile, and that power knows no boundaries of Holy Land. With the coming of Jesus, says Mark the evangelist, the great distinction, the *important* distinction, is no longer the accident of race or nationality, or even the keeping of the law, but faith in Christ, trust in his power to transform life, even to cast out demons and open stopped ears and loose tangled tongues. But the deaf of heart, those who are mute by choice—even the spells of heaven cannot cure their unfaith.

It is hard to believe that half a century ago some Presbyterian churches barred African Americans from membership, or even from entering the door. It is hard to believe that half a century ago all Presbyterian churches barred women from being ordained as ministers, and many, even from exercising leadership on the session. Most institutions in American society were integrated before the churches were. And women were able to exercise leadership roles in a lot of *secular* organizations *long* before Christians finally admitted that Paul's words about there being neither Jew nor Greek, slave nor free, male nor female, must apply even to the church. Where are the lines of distinction today? Who is being excluded today? What barriers between people still remain in the church? The issue of race and nationality has been with the church from its beginnings—witness the great struggle that Paul had with the church leaders in Jerusalem to allow him to minister among the Greeks. The issue of gender has been with the church from its beginnings—witness the need that Paul felt so long ago to teach that there is neither male nor female among those who are in Christ. And then there is the age-old distinction of *class*. Of all the distinctions that have plagued congregations over the years, economic status is the most subtle. Even *ethnic* and *racial* distinctions are not so intractable as distinctions of wealth, and in America, a lot of our ethnic and racial distinctions really hinge as much on economic class as they do on color of skin and accent of speech. It is subtle, for it is something that can be communicated with a glance, with a phrase, with a choice of where to sit in the sanctuary or at the fellowship dinner. It is fatal to the soul that makes the distinction, for it shows contempt for God's precious creation in his own image. It is fatal to the church that permits the distinction to be made, for it shows that the church honors something much more highly than it honors the Christ who was born in the stable, the Christ who spent the night in the fields and the garden, the Christ who was laid in the borrowed tomb.

"You do well if you really fulfill the royal law according to the scripture, 'You shall love your neighbor as yourself,'" says the letter of James. "But if you show partiality, you commit sin and are convicted by the law as transgressors" (Jas 2:8–9 NRSV). And loving our neighbor in theory—a prayer and a word of encouragement now and then and a token at Thanksgiving and Christmas—isn't enough. "If a brother or sister is naked and lacks daily food, and one of you says to them, 'Go in peace; keep warm and eat your fill,' and yet you do not supply their bodily needs, what is the good of that?" (2:15–16 NRSV). It is a matter of faith without works, and faith without works is pointless. In fact, faith without works—faith that is not constantly expressed in faithful deeds, and especially deeds for those who are God's particular concern according to scripture, the poor and the outcast, the foreigner and the sojourner—such faith is not really faith at all.

I was disturbed once to be asked by someone (not in this congregation), "Do you mean to say that we should impoverish ourselves?" The person was referring to something I had written about the Christian imperative to *share* what God has given us for the benefit of others. How often, when wanting to discredit somebody for suggesting something that makes us uncomfortable, we immediately rush to the extreme and try to show the absurdity of the idea. No, I didn't say that, and I don't think God says that, although a lot of people throughout Christian history have felt compelled to *do* just that—to impoverish themselves—in order to be faithful to God's priorities. Jesus told a rich young man to sell all that he possessed and give the proceeds to the poor, because that was the only way that *that* individual would truly be able to follow Christ. Jesus must have been pleased to hear that a tax collector in Jericho, despised by his neighbors, gave half of his possessions away to the poor. Jesus had wealthy friends. There is no reason to imagine that Jesus rebuked Joseph of Arimathea for being rich. Paul had wealthy friends. He did not condemn Barnabas for his prosperity, which went a long way in bringing the gospel to Asia. But Jesus was wealthiest of all—not in money or possessions, of course, but in the sense that he had the most to give. And by his example of generosity, with love and mercy and compassion and hope, the *wealthy* around him, and countless wealthy who have since pledged to *follow* him, have learned to be generous with *their* riches, quietly and as a matter of course. *That* is what wealth is for, in Christian teaching—to give away, to benefit those who are without. Stockpiling large amounts for a rainy day shows a lack of trust in God's goodness. Sharing freely with others shows that God the Father of our Lord Jesus Christ rules *our* hearts, not Mammon. And what is true for *individual* Christians is certainly true for *churches*.

We were all impressed a dozen years ago this week with the tremendous outpouring of admiration and grief for Lady Diana, princess of Wales, and the long silence of Buckingham Palace. I think the great lesson to be learned by the British royalty is the common people's longing that those who are their social superiors not treat them with contemptuous disregard. Diana was the one member of the royal household at the time who showed obvious affection for the common person, was comfortable in the presence of the lowliest beggar, reached out to the most desperately sick, embraced the most gruesomely disfigured. She was the only one who *seemed*, at least, not to allow *her* great *wealth* and *another* person's great *poverty* to affect the way that she treated that person. If that fact is a critique of the monarch as head of *state*, it is even *more* of a critique of the monarch as head of the nation's *church*. For it is the church that should show in its own life and witness what God wants all of creation to be. It is the church that should object most insistently against distinctions of gender and race and nationality and class. It is the church that should demonstrate most emphatically the commonality of *all* people as sinners, *all* people as dependent solely upon divine grace, *all* people as unworthy of salvation, *all* people as loved by God beyond measure. It all begins *here*—or it *should*. And so we were impressed also with the tremendous outpouring of admiration and grief for Mother Teresa, who brought to the world's attention and the attention of the Christian church more dramatically than any other figure of modern times the wretchedness of the poor and the outcast, and their claim upon those of us who live in comfort and plenty. Hers was a lonely witness to the church that being a *follower* of Jesus Christ means bearing the *cross* of Jesus Christ and doing the *ministry* of Jesus Christ.

Has the church been the *first* organization to erase distinctions between peoples, or is it one of the *last*? Is the church the place where people of *different* social status and incomes and colors and languages and customs and clothing and abilities meet and mix and share most freely, and then carry that love and mercy and generosity out into the world? Or are churches often known for being the places where family feuds are perpetuated and those who are different are condemned, where miserliness is more common than generosity and privilege is practiced more often than servanthood? Sadly, that was the case in the church that James knew.

It all begins here. It begins with what is preached from the pulpit. It begins with what is experienced in the sacraments. It begins with what is taught in the classroom. It begins with how we relate to each other in the sanctuary and in the fellowship hall. It begins with focusing not on maintaining the church as an institution, but with focusing on the only reason that the institution exists—to carry on Christ's ministry of welcoming and forgiving and comforting and healing and feeding and bringing to faith all people, regardless of pedigree, regardless of net worth, regardless of gender, regardless of what side of the border they're from. It spills over to our family worship and family Bible reading and family prayer time. And from there it spreads out in the way we conduct our business, treat our employees and fellow workers, our neighbors from the wealthiest to the poorest, of every race and nationality, of both genders, and do the work of government, which the Bible says is principally caring for the poor and the sick and the dispossessed. The church should not be the *last* place to expect mercy and justice and generosity and hope. It should be the *first* place. It should all begin here.

Whatever the circumstances of that exchange between Jesus and the Syrophoenician woman, the fact that it is in the Gospel indicates that Mark, divinely inspired, wanted *his* church to know that there is no longer *any* excuse for barriers between people, for withholding compassion, for failing to share. *James's* church had not learned that lesson. Now, Mark's Gospel addresses *us*. If the world is ever to fulfill God's will that all people are entitled to hope and dignity and mercy and a full share of creation's bounty, we need always to remember that it all begins *here*.

Twenty-Fourth Sunday in Ordinary Time

Spanish Springs Presbyterian Church, Sparks, Nevada
September 17, 2000

Proverbs 1:20–33
James 3:1–12
Mark 8:27–38

"Words on Words"

YOU AND I ARE part of a culture in which words are cheap. We are bombarded by words. They are like a daily tidal wave. They come thick at us by the hundreds, by the thousands. Television. Radio. Internet. Cell phone. "Attention, shoppers." "Attention, passengers." "Attention, you who just thought you could have a quiet family mealtime." And the more *competition* there is for our attention, the less attention we *give*. And the less attention we *get*, the more we *talk*. We have to be speaking or listening to words all the time. Now we even have little machines that allow us to speak or listen to words anywhere, anytime—words sung, some of them pretty trashy; words spoken, some of them pretty shallow—and we dutifully respond to the beep or the buzzer just like Pavlov's dogs. In checkout lines. At the playground. While we should be driving. So many words.

But words can still be influential. Anyone who doubts the impact of words, and the truth of what the letter of James says about the power of words, simply hasn't been paying attention to the news this week. A vulgarism uttered by a presidential candidate into the ear of a vice-presidential candidate and into a live microphone, an uncomplimentary word or part of a word flashed across television screens in a political ad, one too many hostile words said by a college basketball coach with a hot temper, and you pretty much have the summary of this past week's headlines, don't you? Remarkably, there have been no apologies, as if words really *don't* matter, and, if ignored, words will soon be forgotten. "Born-again" candidates suddenly sound just like people who don't know what the phrase "born again" even means. And in the case of a college basketball coach, the reaction of students and alumni suggests that having a civil tongue and a civil demeanor, modeling civility for young people, teaching good manners to young people and respect for others, is far less important than having a winning team—or at least a team that scores more points than the *other* team.

There is no question that words are cheap in our contemporary society. We have come not to believe what people say in advertising. We have come to distrust what people say in politics. Many people have come to doubt even what ministers and priests and rabbis say. But let's look even closer to home. With divorce so common, spouses wonder whether they can trust the words that they said to each other at their weddings. And the cynicism of the teenage years probably has something to do with how often parents tell their children to behave one way and then demonstrate just the opposite in their own behavior. Many years ago, a comedian built his routine around his claim that words have no real importance. When he uttered a series of obscenities in his night-club act, he was arrested. But since those days the courts have essentially sided with his view, so that now just about any words are spoken just about anywhere, appear on billboards and bumper stickers and T-shirts and over the airwaves and the Internet. Well, the Supreme Court reasoned, if you are offended by them, just turn them off, or avert your eyes. Freedom of expression is superior to freedom from disgust. But where *can* you turn these days? Where *can* you look? What television or radio program doesn't spew profanities and obscenities out by the dozen, and their ratings go up? And, worst of all, perhaps, we are no longer shocked by it.

I remember the first time I heard someone swearing. I was in a farm implement store in Minneapolis, Kansas. I was almost twelve years old. There was an old farmer sitting there who struck up a conversation with my step-grandfather, and the man couldn't utter a single sentence without a profanity in it. There's no excuse for such language in any setting, of course, but at least you didn't used to hear it in public—surely not around women and children. Two summers ago, on our way back from the Hymn Society meeting in Vancouver, twelve-year-old Christy and I landed at the airport in Eugene, Oregon, to spend the night. While we were waiting to be picked up by a motel courtesy van, a couple of men who had just landed in a business jet walked into the lobby and remained there in loud conversation that featured a popular obscenity in each sentence, sometimes several times in each sentence. Christy and I couldn't go anywhere—we had to stay there in order to be picked up by the van. I finally asked them to exercise some restraint for the sake of my little girl. They looked at me like I was speaking Swahili—didn't have a clue what I was referring to. Last Saturday morning, Fred and Lou and I were walking door to door handing out flyers and inviting people to worship God with us. As I was walking back to my car to get some more brochures, I passed one of the houses we had just visited, and I heard a father standing in the driveway complaining loudly to his young boys, Jesse's age or younger, that they were not properly dressed for going to the football game that afternoon, in words that literally condemned his children to an eternity in hell. And even many church people these days use the sacred names God and Jesus and Christ as expletives—even clergy, sometimes, I guess, in a misdirected effort to show that we're just regular guys and gals. No wonder children even the age of our little Beth can be heard on the playground swearing; they had to have learned that from somewhere. We think that words don't matter.

But there's a lot of evidence to the contrary. The Bible considers words to have power, so that simply uttering a word goes a long way toward bringing about what the word represents. "In the beginning was the Word . . . . And God said . . . . And it was so." Not only *God's* words, but the words of *human* characters in the Bible had dramatic effects. Remember how Jacob had tricked his father into giving him the blessing that the father had intended for Jacob's brother, Esau. But when the mistake was revealed, his father had no way of retracting the words of blessing that he had spoken to the wrong son. In fact, words *do* have *lasting* effects, on adults as well as children. And the *wrong* words have *damaging* effects, *devastating* effects. Words can cause wars—sometimes even words spoken or written generations ago. Words can disrupt families. In marriage counseling, it usually does not take very long before one of the spouses brings into *today's* disagreement something hurtful that was said *years before*. And political careers have been ruined by words spoken in jest or in haste or in ignorance.

I can't think of a single commandment that ought to be easier to keep than the *Third* Commandment—"You shall not make wrongful use of the name of the Lord your God" (Exod 20:7a NRSV). But in fact there is truth to what James implies—the tongue is the most difficult part of the body to keep disciplined. "Anyone who makes no mistakes in speaking is perfect," says James, "able to keep the whole body in check with a bridle" (Jas 3:2b NRSV). But none of us *is* perfect, "[f]or," as James admits to his Christian audience, "all of us make many mistakes" (3:2a NRSV). Which isn't to say that making many mistakes in speaking or any other activity is OK or even excusable. "If we put bits into the mouths of horses to make them obey us, we guide their whole bodies. Or look at ships: though they are so large that it takes strong winds to *drive* them, yet they are *guided* by a very small rudder wherever the will of the pilot directs. So also the tongue is a small member, yet it boasts of great exploits"—destroying relationships, dismantling reputations, blaspheming God. "How great a forest is set ablaze by a small fire! And the tongue is a fire" (3:3-6a NRSV). So we mustn't deceive ourselves that we can isolate our locker-room talk from our sanctuary talk, that it's all right to speak one way in Sunday school and to speak another way in the office, that we can separate our conversation in the snack bar from our prayers at the communion table. Did you catch the irony in that passage from James? "With [our tongue] we *bless* the Lord and Father, and with it we *curse* those who are made in the *likeness of God*. From the same mouth come blessing and cursing. My brothers and sisters, this ought not to be so. Does a spring pour forth from the same opening both *fresh* and *brackish* water? Can a *fig* tree, my brothers and sisters, yield *olives*, or a grapevine *figs*? No more can *salt* water yield *fresh*" (3:9-12 NRSV). No *genuine praise* of God, James is saying, can come from lips that *curse* or *slander* God's *creation*, a fellow human being. God will not accept the words of adoration that we wedge in between our words of condemnation.

James's message was directed especially at those who are or want to be preachers and teachers in the church. They bear a heavy responsibility, and God will judge *their* words accordingly. Better to speak less and listen more. Perhaps the congregation James was most concerned about was endangered by people who were teaching false doctrine, or whose words were contradicted by their behavior. But James made the more general point that if someone's religion doesn't give that person any control over the tongue, so that her or his words will edify and not corrupt, then that person's religion is useless. It has failed to make any difference at a most fundamental level, and in a behavior from which much damage can result. To speak truly, and to pay attention to what we are saying so that our words *are* true and edifying and gracious and loving—if faith in Jesus Christ doesn't motivate us in *this* way, then does our faith really have any effect on our lives *at all*? Not that we are perfect—James admits that—or that we can live faithfully without the help of the Holy Spirit. But think of what it means so casually to damn someone to hell, or to shout at another person in anger the name of the Savior who died for us. Think what it means to speak of God, not in awe and wonder at the goodness of creation and the love and dependability with which God daily provides for us, but with casual disregard, or as a way of shocking others or cursing others. Perhaps the ancient Jews had it right—to avoid misusing the holy name, they decided that they must never speak it at all. They knew the importance of words.

One day, on the way to the region around Caesarea Philippi, Jesus asked his disciples whom they said that he was. What words did they use to identify him? What words expressed what they believed about him, and what words did they speak to represent him to the world? We don't know exactly what happened then, whether there was a period of silence, either awkward or thoughtful, whether a few of the disciples maybe mumbled some tentative responses to Jesus' question, possible answers with question marks at the end of them, like nervous pupils in a classroom who aren't sure they have the answer that the teacher wants to hear. Maybe Peter jumped in immediately, but in a split second or after a long pause, he blurted out, "You are the Messiah" (Mark 8:29b NRSV), perhaps stunning himself as well as the others. And Jesus ordered the disciples not to tell anyone what had been said.

Probably, Jesus was aware that Peter and the others didn't really know what the word meant—"Messiah." They might misuse it, might mislead people into thinking that he was someone different from who he really was, bandied about as the word "Messiah" had been over the centuries. At any rate, it quickly became *clear* that Peter didn't know the meaning of the word, the power of the word, the truth of the word. For when Jesus began to explain that the Messiah would suffer, be rejected, and be killed—I doubt the disciples at that point even heard what Jesus said about rising again after three days—Peter said he mustn't talk that way, mustn't even consider putting himself in such harm's way; maybe Peter was even ashamed of Jesus for thinking such a thing. And then came Jesus' words that were even more shocking to those who had followed him across the lake and through the villages and over the hills for many long months: "If any want to become my followers, let them deny themselves and take up their cross and follow me. For those who want to save their life will lose it, and those who lose their life for my sake, and for the sake of the gospel, will save it" (8:34b–35 NRSV). And he went on to say that anyone who was ashamed of him *and of his words*, well, they would be a tremendous disappointment to Jesus on the last day. Just words, like all those other words we hear and speak so often that they seem almost meaningless? Or words that have an impact, words of power, words of consequence in your life and mine and, through us, in the lives of all the people we know and many we will never meet—words that summon us soberly but single-mindedly to follow Jesus Christ and be his true disciples in everything that we think, in everything that we do, in everything that we say?

Be careful what you say. Let your words be loving. Let your words be constructive. Let your words be truthful. And, at the proper time, let your words be bold. May all the words that come from our lips be an anthem of praise to God and a clear witness to the grace, mercy, and peace that is ours and *all* people's through Jesus Christ.

Twenty-Fifth Sunday in Ordinary Time

First Presbyterian Church, Dodge City, Kansas
September 21, 1997

Proverbs 31:10–31
James 3:13—4:3, 7–8a
Mark 9:30–37

"The Greatest"

RICK GLENVILLE LOOKED INTO the bathroom mirror in his hotel room. His eyes were bloodshot and his hair was disheveled. He had tossed and turned much of the night, though he had been exhausted when he went to bed. And that was after only two and a third innings. But they had been two and a third *long* innings. He had expected to be pulled after he allowed a base hit and then a double, which scored the lead runner. *McClary's fault*, he thought to himself. If that moron of a center fielder had just been where the scouting reports said Holloway would hit an inside fastball, the runner on first wouldn't have gotten past second base. An out, and the pitcher up—an easy out if there ever was one—and he would have fooled Parker into chasing curves for a strikeout to end the inning. But with one run in and a runner on second, Dutch Stevens, the manager of the opposing team, had put in a pinch hitter with a .256 average who drilled Rick Glenville's first pitch over the right-field wall. Rick tried not to look into the dugout, but eventually his eye caught the icy glare of his manager, Tony Bianco. The next batter he faced in his first inning of relief grounded out to shortstop. Then he *hit* the *next* batter for a *walk*, and allowed a double before Sweeney flied out to shallow center.

Bianco, the manager, had continued to glare at him all the way from the mound to the dugout. He had sat down in a heap at the opposite end of the bench, pulling off his glove and dropping it on the bench beside him.

No one said anything to him. Three runs, which wiped out a three-run lead. That's when Glenville's *head* had started to hurt. Was his shoulder hurting, or did he just imagine it? Yeah, his shoulder was hurting by then. He shouldn't be pitching, but he wasn't about to tell the trainer. A reliever who couldn't go in on two days' rest wouldn't have much of a future with *this* club.

His second inning—the seventh—hadn't been any better. Bianco, he knew, didn't have many options, with two of his left-handed relievers on the disabled list and a third held in reserve for a closer. He walked the *first* batter in the seventh, allowed a double, which was followed by a pop fly to deep right, scoring the lead runner, and it went downhill from there. If the pitcher's position had come up in the batting order, he knew, Bianco would have yanked him then and there. But the visit to the mound didn't happen until the lead-off batter in the eighth homered. "You're history" were the only words Bianco said to him as he held out his hand for the ball—words that Glenville imagined summed up Bianco's opinion of his career, not just that night's game.

The telephone rang. Glenville crossed the hotel room to answer it. "Hello," he said.

"It's Lou," said the voice at the other end of the line—the voice that belonged to Lou Vincent, Rick Glenville's agent, who wore loud ties and drove a Cadillac convertible.

"What's it look like?" Rick asked.

"No dice on an increase," Lou said, matter-of-factly, "and that was *before* last night's performance."

"Look," Rick said, "that guy in the sky box is rakin' in the dough. He can afford—"

"It's not a matter of 'afford,'" Lou interrupted him. "It's a matter of 'deliver,' Rick," he said. "They're talkin' *decrease*, and I can't find a single team interested in pickin' you up."

"Listen," Rick said, "someone out there with decent fielders wants a seasoned pitcher."

"All of 'em out there want a *winning* pitcher," Lou corrected him. "You've got to face the facts of your age and your ERA."

"It wasn't that long ago that I had the highest winning percentage in the league," Rick objected, his head starting to hurt again.

"*Three* years ago, and since then, you've been in the steepest tailspin in modern baseball history," said Lou. "I'm doin' my best. But I'm tellin' ya, if you wanna be in a big-league uniform next year, you're gonna haft'a produce or take a cut. And doin' somethin' to court the fans wouldn't hurt."

Glenville muttered a curse and slammed the receiver.

Within seconds, the telephone rang again. "Rick?" the young woman asked after his curt "Hello."

"Yeah," he responded.

"This is Linda in public relations. I've got an appearance for you when you get back to town tomorrow."

"What is it *this* time?" he asked. Normally, Rick Glenville was not so abrupt, but just now his disgust was invading every part of his personality.

"Children's Hospital. A little boy named Miguel."

"*Miguel*?" he asked with a tone of revulsion.

"Miguel Ortega," she answered, ignoring his manner.

"Look," Rick said, "I'm awfully tired after this road trip, and I've got stuff to do tomorrow before practice. Can't you just tell 'em I'm booked up or something? Maybe get someone else to go and take him a taco?"

"The kid's terminal," she said. "The parents say you're his hero."

Rick Glenville was too sore to be a hero just now, even for a *white* kid.

"Are you going to go or not?" Linda wanted to know.

"I'll call you back," he said after a pause, and hung up.

He looked out the window. Where was he? Suddenly, he couldn't remember. What city was this? They had all begun to look alike. What ballpark was he in last night? Green—the outfield walls were dark green. The whole stadium was dark green. It must be Cincinnati. He went back into the bathroom and looked again into the mirror. Thirty-two years old, and he felt like a hundred this morning. Thirty-two years old, and three years after being the winningest starting pitcher in the league, his golden season, he had been relegated to middle reliever. Never had there been such a meteoric rise from promising to outstanding, and never had there been such a dismal decline from outstanding to abysmal. The only thing soaring during the past year was his earned run average, and his innings pitched per game had been declining all season, dramatically, as his team became a serious contender in the division pennant race. But eleven losses in the last fourteen games had knocked them out of contention.

Rick's poor performance was as much a puzzle to himself as it was to analysts like his pitching coach. Deep inside, he knew that the problem wasn't a dumb center fielder. The divorce might have had something to do with it, or losing the starter's designation. No—he realized that his play had been deteriorating even before those things; in fact, his disgust with himself when spring training made clear to everybody that the wonder season was long over had been the *main* thing that *led* to his divorce. "Alone and washed up at thirty-two," he thought to himself. And all he had to show for it was that he was some Mexican kid's hero. "Whoopee," he thought.

He packed his suitcase and took a shower, then dressed and went downstairs for breakfast. Some of the guys were in the coffee shop, but only Dirk Ellis greeted him with more than a grunt. "You look awful," Dirk said as Rick walked past his table. "Why don't you sit down and come back to life with coffee and scrambled eggs?" Rick managed a slight smile and fell into the chair. "They were kind of rough on you last night, weren't they?" asked the backup outfielder.

"Yeah, well, if that idiot McClary—" Rick started, and then waved his hand in a gesture of disdain. Dirk looked at him patiently. "Yeah," Rick spoke again, this time with resignation in his voice, "they hammered me."

"McClary's OK," Dirk said in defense of the starting center fielder for whom Dirk occasionally substituted. "McClary's OK," Dirk said again, now looking at his cup of coffee as he stirred it slowly.

"Yeah," Rick finally said, "McClary's OK. I'm just not sure about Glenville."

"What are you doin' about it?" Dirk asked.

"I've watched video, I've talked with the coaches, I've tried changing my windup, but my fastball's dropped off and my curve isn't foolin' anybody. I've done just about everything but pray."

Rick was surprised that he was being so honest with Dirk, whom he had never regarded particularly as a friend. He was even more surprised when Dirk responded, "Well, then, why don't you pray?"

Rick chuckled, but when Dirk didn't join in, his chuckle trailed off into silence.

Rick's coffee came, and neither man spoke again, then the scrambled eggs and toast, and they ate in silence until Dirk finally commented, "It'll be good to get back home tonight." Dirk lived in a suburb of their team's hometown. Rick was vaguely aware that Dirk had a wife and children—two, he thought, one with some kind of chronic illness.

"Yeah, well, as soon as I get back, I'm s'posed to go see some sick kid in the hospital. Those places give me the creeps. Some Mexican kid."

"It might be a thrill for the kid," Dirk observed coolly.

Rick suddenly remembered that Dirk's wife's name was Maria, and he reddened slightly. "I mean, I don't hold it against him that he's Mexican or anything—" There was an awkward silence. Finally, he thought of a way of trying to take the attention off of his blunder. "This kid thinks I'm hot stuff."

"Then it's up to you not to make him change his mind," Dirk responded icily. The outfielder signed the check, wiped his lips with his napkin, stood up, and left without saying any more.

Rick sat alone for a few minutes, then looked at his watch. Twenty minutes until the team bus left for the ballpark. He went back to his room and telephoned Linda in the public relations office. "I guess I'll go see the kid" was all he said.

As he walked forlornly from the bus to the clubhouse, no one approached Rick for his autograph. No one ever did anymore. Quite a change from three years earlier, or even *one* year earlier. And there was little camaraderie with his teammates these days. He spent that afternoon in the bullpen without ever being called up, or even being told to warm up once the game began. He *could* have pitched, after only a little over two innings the night before. Still, it was an afternoon game—not that many hours since his lackluster performance. The starting pitcher lasted through six innings, giving up only two runs on four hits, and was retired on a pitch count. The telephone in the bullpen rang twice after that, but no one called out Rick's name. Rick's team won by a single run, four to three. Rick tried to sleep on the airplane that evening, but could not.

Rick Glenville nosed his red Pontiac Firebird into a vacant parking spot in the big garage across the street from the hospital. The car had been a gift at the conclusion of his golden season. Now, it was probably the oldest car being driven by anyone on the pitching staff. No one seemed to show any sign of recognition as he walked through the lobby of the hospital toward the bank of elevators, even though he was carrying a baseball in his hand. He pressed the "up" button, and then the button for the fourth floor. The doors opened to reveal a young boy slumped over sideways in a wheelchair with a smile on his face, being pushed by an orderly. At first, Rick thought that the smile was for him, but as he got out of the elevator and the orderly pushed the wheelchair past him into the elevator, he realized that the smile was frozen on the child's face, and the eyes which he *thought* had been looking at *him* had actually been looking *through* him, and then *past* him. Rick cleared his throat and then straightened his tie, and turned left in the direction indicated by the arrow to find room 436.

The little boy in the first bed was asleep. His head was bald, except for a few wisps of very blonde hair above his ears. "This could not be the Ortega kid," Rick thought. He walked farther into the room, and saw behind the curtain separating the beds an Hispanic man in his early- to mid-thirties with anxiety etched in his face. When he glanced up at Rick, his mouth spread into a smile and his eyes filled with tears. "Señor Meester Glenville!" he said, rising from his chair. He turned immediately toward the boy, lying in the bed with an array of bottles hooked up to a shunt in his arm. "Miguel, it's Rick! It's Rick Glenville!"

"Wow!" the boy said with as much enthusiasm as his weak body would allow him. "Is it really *you*?"

On the wall beside the bed, between the window and the IV apparatus, Rick saw a dozen pictures of himself in different poses, from his rookie baseball card to a public relations glossy taken in his golden season. The team pennant was pinned up, and his number was displayed prominently in the middle of the photographs. "Yeah, it's really me," he said after taking in the little shrine to his past glories.

"Dad, it's really him."

The effort to say this brought a convulsion of coughing from the boy, whom Rick judged to be about eleven years old, though it was hard to tell in his emaciated condition. The boy's father bent over his sick child, trying to soothe him. Rick stood clumsily, watching, not knowing what to do. After a minute or so, the coughing fit ended, and the father turned to shake Rick's hand. "This means so much to Miguel," the man said. "I'm Jesse Ortega, and this is Miguel. Ever since we saw you pitch that no-hitter in '94, you've been Miguel's absolutely favorite player. My boss gave me a couple of tickets when we were living down there in Houston and you came to town."

"That was super," Miguel interjected. "I was a big fan of Roberto Chacon, but then you were super."

"He's been your fan ever since," Mr. Ortega explained with a chuckle. "Look," he said, pointing to a baseball sitting on the window sill. "This is the ball that Ramirez hit foul in the bottom of the ninth."

"Everyone thought it was going to be a home run, but it went foul, and I got it, and then he swung and missed on your curveball, and that ended the game," Miguel said, smiling.

"You were sittin' way out there beyond the foul pole?" Rick asked, amazed.

"It's the only time he's been to a real baseball game," Mr. Ortega said. "Ever since we moved *here*, we wanted to come see you at home, but Miguel's been too sick."

"Would you sign the ball?" Miguel asked hopefully.

Rick walked over to the window sill and picked up the ball, turning it over in his fingers, shaking his head. "That was some night," he said, mostly to himself.

"You bet!" said Miguel, his voice bringing Rick back to reality.

"Sure I'll sign it," Rick said, and he sat down on the edge of Miguel's bed and pulled a pen out of his pocket. "In fact, I brought you another ball. I'll sign both of 'em."

Miguel shifted his body a little to make room for his hero, clearly in awe that a Major League pitcher was sitting on *his* bed. "I always wanted to be a first baseman, but now, when I get well, I want to be a pitcher like you," Miguel said. "Maybe I won't be so *good* as you, but almost."

Rick had to turn his head away from the boy for a few seconds, and then he looked back at Miguel and said, "I'm sure you'll be the greatest that ever was." They talked for a few minutes about what it was like that night three years ago in the Astrodome—the no-hitter—and then Mr. Ortega suggested that it was time for Miguel to get some rest. Rick reached over and tousled Miguel's black hair, and the boy beamed. "I'll come back to see ya,'" Rick said.

Mr. Ortega walked out into the hall with him. "Miguel doesn't have much time left, Mr. Glenville," he said. "Maybe not even a week. But the doctors have given their OK for him to go to the game tomorrow afternoon. It's his biggest wish. At this stage, it can't do much harm. His mom's getting off work, and my boss is giving me time off until—" The man's voice broke.

It dawned on Rick that he and Mr. Ortega were about the same age. Rick pulled a card out from his pocket and scribbled a note on it. "If you get to the ballpark, ask for Sandy—head of security. Give him this, and I'll see you after the game."

"Oh, thank you," Mr. Ortega said, and he shook Rick's hand with both of his own.

That night, Rick walked one batter, struck out two, and gave up a double. Tony Bianco, the manager, said nothing to him. But the next day, Rick approached the manager on his own initiative. "Tony," he said.

"Yeah, what is it?"

"I sure hope you'll call on me this afternoon."

"You weren't exactly brilliant last night."

"I can do you some good today—I know it. Please, just let me try. It's really important to me. I know I haven't been so hot. But please."

Tony looked at him a long time, his lips pursed. Finally, he answered, "Your arm's OK?"

"Yeah, Tony, my arm's OK."

"Well, we'll see."

By the top of the seventh inning, Rick's hopes were fading. His team was behind by four runs, when Mickey McGuinn drove in two more runs on a line drive deep to right center field, which McClary couldn't handle. The phone rang in the bullpen. Rick got the call. With his heart in his throat, he trotted out to the mound.

"Don't make me regret this," Bianco said to him at the mound, but Rick realized that, six runs down, Bianco probably figured he had nothing to lose by calling on him. The first batter he faced flied out to end the top of the inning.

Rick's teammates scored two runs in the bottom of the seventh, thanks in part to his own well-executed sacrifice bunt. In the top of the eighth, Rick allowed two singles, but got out of the inning without a run being scored. *His* team, however, scored three quick runs in the bottom of the eighth. It was a one-run ballgame. Then another run. And another. When the eighth inning was over, Rick's team had a one-run lead.

Rick looked down the bench at Tony Bianco and saw the agony on the manager's face. "Well," Bianco finally barked at him, "get out there."

Rick's heart pounded as he walked out to the mound and he heard a chorus of "Boos" criticizing Bianco's decision to keep him in the game. As the first batter was approaching the plate, Rick searched the stands for a little black-haired boy, but could not see him. He did not quite know how he did it, but he struck out the first batter on three successive fastballs. His first pitch to the next batter was a ball, but then he got him to reach down for a breaking ball, which he hung up for the third baseman to catch with ease.

Two outs, and the sweat was pouring from Rick Glenville. The "Boos" had become cheers, but then he made a mistake, and the next batter lifted his curveball into deep center field, where McClary bumbled it, turning an *out* into a *triple*. Rick looked into the dugout at Bianco, but Bianco just looked down at his feet. Rick *walked* the next batter on a strike and then four straight balls. The "Boos" were deafening. Still no indication from Bianco. And then, as if by magic, a foul, a called strike, and a swung-on strike. The ballpark erupted. Rick's teammates swarmed and smothered him, but he broke free and ran toward the gated steps that descended alongside the dugout from the box seats to the playing field.

Fans reached out to shake his hand, but Rick craned his neck looking for one fan in particular. After two or three minutes, he saw Mr. Ortega pushing through the throng, carrying Miguel in his arms, followed by a woman whom Rick took to be Miguel's mother. "Hooray!" Mr. Ortega said. Or was it "Olé"? Rick could not tell.

Miguel's tired little face had a broad grin. "How was that, Miguel?" Rick asked the boy, gently laying his hand on the boy's arm, which was resting on his stomach, and then reaching over the gate to take Miguel into his own arms.

As Miguel settled into Rick's embrace, the boy looked up and answered, "You're the greatest."

Twenty-Sixth Sunday in Ordinary Time

First Presbyterian Church, Ponca City, Oklahoma
September 27, 2015

Esther 7:1–6, 9–10; 9:20–22
James 5:13–20
Mark 9:38–50

"Life Woven into God"

THE PAPAL VISIT TO the United States this week has turned the nation's attention to matters of religion in a way that, for many of us, is at least a refreshing diversion from the caustic political circus that has been debasing our public conversation and corroding the fabric of our country. Perhaps like no other pope since John XXIII, Francis is being perceived as a person whose faith is transparent and constant. He gives evidence at every opportunity of someone whose *manner* is wholly consistent with his *beliefs*, and whose *beliefs* are at the core of his *being*. And, while he has shown no intention of changing Catholic dogma, Pope Francis interprets the church's teaching as flowing out of *life with God*, not as a threat of *damnation*; a *call* to embrace the *love of God*, not a tool of *coercion*. His recent invitation to include people who have been divorced, women who have had abortions, lesbians and gays—all people popularly long considered *unwelcome* in the Roman Catholic Church—seems totally consistent with a gospel of love, even though he shows no intention of altering the church's disapproval of divorce and abortion and homosexuality.

While you and I and other Christians may disagree with the official Roman Catholic stance on these and other issues, we can applaud Francis's acknowledgment that *judgment* is up to *God*, and that *none* of us knows perfectly the *mind* of God, and that what we *do* know is *Jesus Christ*. Without at all compromising God's will, Jesus nonetheless always put the divine purpose of redeeming all of creation at the top of his agenda, even to the point of sacrificing his own life in obedience to God. Jesus never dismissed *sin*, but he also never dismissed the *sinner*. He testified that behind every *rule* in the Bible is the love of God, merciful and redeeming.

What is true of *Jesus* should also be true of the *church*. The rules established by God must be taken *seriously*, but the reason is that God takes our *salvation* seriously. God does not ignore sin. But sin will never be the last word in God's creation. God calls us to see everything from God's perspective as we know it in Christ. God calls us to live fully embraced by God's love. That means that every deed we do, every word we say, every thought we have, will naturally and instinctively express God's very own love. Pope Francis, I think, wants all people—Catholic and non-Catholic, Christian and non-Christian—to understand that.

The twelve disciples of Jesus had the precious opportunity of three years in Jesus' earthly company to understand it. But even *they* thought faith was largely a matter of prerogative and judgment, privilege and exclusion. One day, Mark the evangelist tells us, the twelve happened to witness a man who wasn't one of their number casting out demons in Jesus' name—the only name in which demons *could* be cast out. To do something in Jesus' name means not just saying the word "Jesus," but having the same *motive* as Jesus and doing things in the same *manner* as Jesus. Just a few verses earlier, Mark told of an episode of *Jesus* casting out an unclean spirit from a boy who had been convulsed by the demon, and who had fallen on the ground and was rolling about and foaming at the mouth.

Surely, Mark wanted his readers to remember how *Jesus* had exorcised the unclean spirit from the boy when, now just a few verses *later*, he told that the disciples complained to Jesus that they had seen someone who *wasn't* one of his disciples doing the *same thing*. Sandwiched between these two astounding episodes is the sad story that we read last Sunday, about the disciples arguing among themselves who was the greatest, the preeminent, the favored. Jesus had responded to the disciples' argument by telling them that *his* followers must be *servants of others*, and not *worry* about their authority and prestige. And now, in reply to their rather self-righteous suggestion that only the *official* followers of Jesus should enjoy the privilege of casting out demons, Jesus said, "Whoever is not *against* us is *for* us. For truly I tell you, whoever gives you a cup of water to drink because you bear the name of Christ will by no means lose the reward" (Mark 9:40–41 NRSV). And then he went on to tell them, speaking of water, that it would be better for a person to be thrown into the sea with a heavy weight around his neck than to be the reason that another person should miss the kingdom of God.

And he ended his teaching by saying that the disciples should have a zesty faith and be at peace with one another.

That's quite a range of subject matter in just a few verses, but it all has at its root a challenge, I think, to the popular supposition that being a follower of Jesus Christ is about being in the club, and knowing the secret handshake, and not violating its checklist of behavior, at least not egregiously. Christianity, and Judaism before it, has often been thought of as a set of *rules*—if you do *this*, then you're *in*, and if you do *that*, then you're *out*. If you profess your faith in *these* words, then you are *accepted*, and if you *don't*, then you are *excluded*. And even *that* has been too often reduced to supposing that if you reserve an hour a week for God in your life (unless something else comes up), then you are satisfying the requirement.

But Jesus, here in our reading, dashes any notion of exclusiveness by way of keeping rules and preserving privilege, and any notion that faithfulness to God is like a garment we can put on and take off. If Christians or the church fail to be motivated by the gospel of love at *all* times, if Christians or the church bless violence or prejudice at *any* time, if Christians or the church should covet prestige or practice dominance over *anyone*, if Christians or the church should prove to be just an extension of social status and yet another example of class division, then Christians and the church are turning people away from the kingdom of God and showing that theirs is an *insipid* faith, at best—one without any appeal.

Rather than rejoicing that a demon-possessed person had been freed from an unclean spirit, the disciples were grumbling that the miracle had been performed by someone who was outside the club. That's pretty much the same complaint that the Pharisees and priests and scribes had against *Jesus*. "Do not stop him" (9:39a NRSV), Jesus ordered them. At that moment, by curing the person who was afflicted, that *non*-disciple showed himself to be in truth nearer to the heart of God than the *disciples* were. *They* had earlier tried to exorcise the *same* demon from the *same* boy and had utterly *failed*! So now they jealously wanted to guard and preserve their exclusive status of being the authorized assistants of Jesus, even if it meant people therefore went uncured!

But that was not God's will, and it wasn't Jesus' gospel. The disciples' concerns about authority and privilege were closing the gates of the kingdom to people *God* wanted to *include*. They were all anxious to safeguard a faith that had lost its substance. They were all concerned to place ministry to others in the category of a correct "religious" answer to human need that had little room for spontaneous, uncalculated servanthood. Caution, control, approval, permission were the watchwords of their faith—faith that was like salt that had lost its saltiness, faith that ultimately can be restricted, limited, measured, rationed, faith that finds expression for no more than a single hour on a Sunday, faith that thinks the goal is to plug God into a hole in *our* lives, rather than weaving *our* lives into the fullness of *God*. The *non*-disciple had behaved in a way that was closer to the heart of God than what the twelve *disciples* were doing, for he had restored to wholeness a young life whom a demon was trying to wreck.

The lives of the disciples, it seems, were not yet woven into the life of God—into the loving priorities and redeeming rhythms of the kingdom of which they were supposed to be living advertisements and devoted ambassadors. Their minds were very much on worldly considerations. Their eyes saw only what was physically visible, not the truth that was beyond touch and sight. When they asked Jesus why *they* had been *unable* to exorcise the demon from the boy, Jesus had told them that it required prayer. Hadn't they even *prayed* for the man whom the *non*-disciple had helped? "The prayer of faith will save the sick," James explained, "and the Lord will raise them up; and anyone who has committed sins will be forgiven" (Jas 5:15 NRSV).

The task of the Christian is not first and foremost to live by codes and draw a circle around oneself to exclude those who *don't*. The task of the Christian is first and foremost to weave his or her life into the fullness of God. Jesus' ministry was not about compiling a list of do's and don'ts. Jesus' ministry was a demonstration of the kingdom of God in all of its truth, all of its generosity, all of its hospitality, all of its priority over the world's ways of greed and lust and envy and prejudice and pride. And Jesus was able to *do* that because Jesus' life was so completely woven into the life of God that Jesus' blessing was *God's* blessing, Jesus' forgiveness was *God's* forgiveness, Jesus' command was *God's* command; or, perhaps more correctly, God's *blessing* was what *Jesus* spoke, God's *forgiveness* was what *Jesus* offered, God's *command* was the call to faithfulness that *Jesus* echoed with every gesture and every word.

Does every deed you do and the way you do it, does every word you say and the way you say it, weave you more firmly and seamlessly into the life of God, who loves the world so much that he gave his only Son, humble and willing to suffer, merciful and refusing to return evil for evil, that it might have true life?—life here and now and for all eternity, life that is defined not by condemnation and exclusion but by the depth and breadth of God's embrace. Is your life so gently and graciously woven into God that words of prayer flow easily from your lips, *and* words of blessing, and works of mercy are worked easily by your hands, *and* works of generosity? Do you rise to greet the new day as an opportunity to live in God's love and show thanksgiving for it by loving others and sharing with them God's abundance? Is the merciful and generous love of God filling your mind when you go into the voting booth? Is God's concern for the poor and dignity for every human being and value of every part of creation filling your mind when you go down the grocery aisle. or when you read or hear of the headline issues of the day, from immigration to healthcare to pollution? Are these things for which God's purpose is *irrelevant* in your daily living and the choices you make? Or is *your* life with *God* such that *nothing* in your daily experience and decision process is *beyond* your faith or *disconnected* from your faith? Is God the constant reality in whom you live and move and have your being? Is your life woven into God?

No one is perfect—only God, and Jesus Christ his Son. But in the past few days, I have been more and more impressed with what a life lived in reflection on divine perfection can look like. And I think that *all* of us, Catholic and non-Catholic, clergy and laity, can be thankful that, in our lifetime, we have been blessed with such a winsome example of one who has salt in himself and seeks ways to be at peace with others—someone who encourages *us* to weave *our* lives into *God*.

Twenty-Seventh Sunday in Ordinary Time

First Presbyterian Church, Dodge City, Kansas
October 5, 1997

Job 1:1; 2:1–10
Hebrews 1:1–4; 2:5–12
Mark 10:2–16

"Are You Too Grown Up for the Kingdom?"

Now, GOD HAS SENT his Son. The author of the letter to the Hebrews announced in the first few sentences the theme of his letter: the former revelations through the prophets were incomplete, were imperfect, but *now* God has provided the genuine key to the true meaning of life and to the destiny of every human being and of all humankind. Now, God has sent his Son, and the cosmic Christ meets us from within our own humanity—our own feelings, our own yearnings, our own needs, our own limitations. Now, God has sent his Son, and the risen Lord of the universe is the same one who understands our human condition—our fears, our temptations, our perplexities, our suffering. Inspired though they were, the prophets could only tell *about* God. The Son is in his very nature and being the complete revelation of God himself. To see the *Son* is to see *God*. To hear the *Son* is to hear *God*. To obey the *Son* is to obey *God*. God and the Son are *that close*. And the Son dared openly to call God "*the Father.*"

Great theological battles have been fought in the Christian church during the course of its history over exactly what it means to say that Jesus is the Son of God. The official answer came in the early 300s with the approval of the Nicene Creed by a great council of the church. It says that Jesus Christ is of the same substance with the Father, by whom all things were made. But that did not really settle the issue, for our human language is so inadequate to express divine mystery, and our human reasoning is so insufficient to probe divine truth. So volumes have been written in an attempt to unpack the meaning of the identity of Jesus the Son and his relationship to God the Father. Quite rightly, feminists and others have reminded us that no *human* conception of fatherhood or even parenthood is adequate to describe God. And yet, Jesus found that word—"Father"—the best expression of who *God* was to *him*, and found that word—"Son," "child"—the best expression of who *he* was to *God*. And Jesus bequeathed to his followers that *same* language and that *same* relationship with God, teaching his disciples to address God the *same way* when praying together, "Our Father . . ."

Actually, the word that Jesus used was not quite so formal as our English word "Father," which is more about the *biological* relationship or the *role* of the male parent than a *name* to call someone. The word that Jesus seems to have used, *Abba*, was the Aramaic word that was preferred in *family* circles, around the house. It is more along the lines of "Dad," or "Daddy." It is not the language of theologians. It is not the language of lawyers. It is the language of a young child—unsophisticated, unconcerned with propriety, oblivious to etiquette, knowing only love and familiarity and trust.

We in our modern Western culture tend to romanticize childhood. There was a time in our own American history when children were brought into the world as much to provide extra hands around the farm or the shop as to be showered with affection. It has not been very long that children have been regarded as persons in their *own* right, individuals whose opinions are considered worthy of adult respect and whose welfare is considered worthy of legal protection. A century and more ago, law and society accorded children no independent rights. The words in traditional weddings about "giving away the bride" date back to the English common-law days when a daughter, like a son, was considered to be the *property* of a father, pretty much in the same category as a plow or a horse. That is why our Presbyterian wedding service discourages "giving away the bride"; the thought of the daughter being the father's property is not compatible with our understanding that a man and woman should come to the decision themselves to be husband and wife, as free individuals and without compulsion, as people in the image of God acting of their own will, making their own choices and commitments. The church has an obligation not to reinforce by its words and its actions those things that are contrary to the Christian faith. In the time of Jesus, children had no status or power, no protection of the law, no consideration when it came to making family decisions—and especially girls, who could not choose when and whom to marry, who did not even figure as heirs. So it is remarkable that Jesus would be remembered as having addressed *God* as a *child* would address his or her "Daddy," and it was remarkable that Jesus took time for and showed interest in children, who were unimportant to most people around him, including even his disciples.

In fact, one day, when Jesus was talking about very grown-up things like God's intentions for marriage and the way that divorce contradicts God's *purpose* for marriage, some people, probably mothers or nannies, brought some children to Jesus hoping that he would touch them, apparently in blessing, and his disciples rebuked them for doing so. Scripture does not say *why* the disciples were unhappy to have the children pushed toward Jesus, but, given the general attitude of that culture toward children, it probably had to do with their perceived insignificance. Jesus had more important things to do than be bothered with the kids, they must have thought. Jesus needed to spend *his* attention on *serious* matters, they must have reasoned. The place where the grown-ups were gathered to talk about God or any other subject was not a proper place for children, they must have believed.

"But when Jesus saw this, he was indignant and said to them, 'Let the little children come to me; do not stop them; for it is to such as these that the kingdom of God belongs'" (Mark 10:14 NRSV). There are a lot of sermons in that sentence—serious matters like whether a congregation is spending its money and providing inviting classrooms and offering themselves as teachers in a way that demonstrates that the church believes children are important; serious matters like whether Christian parents are overprogramming their children with sports and other activities to the point that there is no time left for spiritual instruction and church fellowship; serious matters like whether the adult generation is providing a model, in its vocabulary and its attitudes and its behaviors, that truly and unambiguously teaches youth who Jesus is and what obedience to Jesus means. But this morning, I want to focus on the *next* sentence of Jesus: "'Truly I tell you, whoever does not receive the kingdom of God as a little child will never enter it.' And [Jesus] took [the children] up in his arms, laid his hands on them, and blessed them" (10:15–16 NRSV).

The disciples were trying to enforce the accepted social custom, trying to keep the lessons of the teacher and his students from being disrupted by childish prattle and misbehavior. As I said, childhood was not romanticized in Jesus' time. The word "child" brought to mind unruliness, not cuteness; mischief, not innocence; another mouth to feed, not a future president. But when Jesus said, "[W]hoever does not receive the kingdom of God as a little child will never enter it" (10:15 NRSV), the very point he was making had to do with a child's *lack* of rights, *lack* of status, *lack* of claim for any consideration of privilege or prestige. A child was totally dependent upon her or his parent—in those days, her or his *father*—not only for food and shelter and clothing, but for whatever status or power the child might ever hope for—even for whether the child lived or died. The child could claim *nothing* by virtue of simply being born, had *no* rights of his or her own, but was *totally* at the mercy of "Daddy."

"[W]hoever does not receive the kingdom of God as a little child will never enter it" (10:15 NRSV). Whoever does not give up all claim of *right* to God's grace shall not enter the kingdom. Whoever does not abandon all normal human calculations of *greatness* shall not enter the kingdom. Whoever is not radically and entirely dependent upon *God* for status, for inheritance, for life itself, shall not enter the kingdom. Whoever thinks that *he* or *she* can set the conditions for entering the kingdom will be totally disappointed. That is what Jesus said to the adult male disciples who were shoving away the children, the "non-persons." Once again, the disciples had entirely missed the point of everything that Jesus had been teaching them. Once again, they had been blind to his actions and deaf to his words, and had thought that the blessings of Jesus were meant for the inner group, for those who had status, for those who were worthy, for those already in the club. Once again, they failed to understand and practice the radical and scandalous inclusiveness of the gospel, of the welcome that Jesus extends, and commands his *followers* to extend, to the wretched and the despised and the outcast, the "non-person"—whether it be the child in Jesus' day or the homeless street person in our day, whether the leper or the AIDS victim, whether the harlot or the homosexual, whether the Gentile or the undocumented alien.

There are people in our sanctuary, I know, who are horrified at the suggestion of addressing God as "Daddy." Only King James English will do. Only "Father," in bold and masculine script, is appropriate to God's majesty, to God's power, to God's authority, to God's holiness. We may even be a little chagrined that on the occasion when Jesus prayed in the garden, pleading that God remove from him the cup of suffering, the spectre of the cross of torture and execution, even the Greek Gospel of Mark specifies that Jesus addressed God as *Abba*, as "Dad" or "Daddy." But is it really *God's majesty* that is in jeopardy, or is it *our sophistication*? Is it that it strikes us as *disrespectful*, or is it that we don't take so literally that in Jesus Christ we *too are children of God*? Is it that we don't want to *offend* God, or is it that we really don't like the idea of being completely and totally and utterly *dependent* upon God for everything in our life? Is it that we don't want to presume *too much*, or is it that we don't want just *anybody*—even the *non-persons* of our *own* society—to feel *that familiar* with the God whose salvation *we* think has to be *earned*?

Are *you* too grown up for the kingdom of God?—too caught up in thinking that a paycheck is the measure of worthiness, too caught up in thinking that heaven has to do with obeying rules, too caught up in the weight of responsibilities that really don't matter much when you compare them with the salvation of your soul, and that tend to make you think that you yourself can prevent disaster or prolong your life or earn God's blessings? Or are you still *childlike* in your thoughts and your words and your actions, in your trust and your hope and your love, confessing and demonstrating unashamedly that your *reputation*, your *prosperity*, your *salvation*, your very *life*, are all owing to nothing more and nothing less than the undeserved grace of God, for which you are so thankful and joyful that your gratitude and your joy radiate out toward others? It is not easy, in a culture that wants you to think *its* thoughts of success, that wants you to esteem *its* measures of wealth, that wants you to draw lines of distinction between *your deserving* and *others' undeserving*. It is not normal, in a society that condemns dependence, that judges the poor, that ridicules the powerless. But it is what Jesus said is necessary. "'Truly I tell you, whoever does not receive the kingdom of God as a little child will never enter it.' And he took them up in his arms, laid his hands on them, and blessed them" (10:15–16 NRSV).

Twenty-Eighth Sunday in Ordinary Time

Spanish Springs Presbyterian Church, Sparks, Nevada
October 12, 2003

Job 23:1–9, 16–17
Hebrews 4:12–16
Mark 10:17–31

"Stripped-Down Faith"

LOST AMONG THE HEADLINES of recall election, the failure to find weapons of mass destruction, and the leaking of the identity of a CIA agent, a rather remarkable story has been playing out in the state of Alabama. Alabama is one of the poorest states in the nation, with a high proportion of its citizens living below the official poverty line. The governor of that state, self-described as an evangelical and, I take it, fundamentalist Christian, and belonging to a political party known for its resistance to taxes and its championing of business interests, has announced that he has found the state's tax structure to be immoral. The tax structure, he has come to believe, weighs much too heavily on people of low income while taxing corporations, including the state's giant timber industry, too lightly. The governor has come to his conclusion, he says, based on his reading of scripture, and scripture's commands to *care for* and *not burden* the *poor*. His reading of the Bible has prompted him to call for an increase of taxes upon the wealthy and upon large corporate profits and real estate holdings, and a decrease or elimination of taxes upon the state's poorest citizens.

Those who would be the target for increased taxation are furious, and a spokesperson for the Christian Coalition has publicly denied any connection between the Bible and appropriate tax policy, or any biblical mandate for government even to be concerned about the poor. He and the governor don't seem to be reading the same Bible—I certainly don't think that he could be reading the book of Leviticus or Deuteronomy or the Psalms and the Old Testament prophets, like the governor has been doing. A lot of people are in shock that a politician has actually linked matters of wealth and poverty and taxes to the Bible. Given the political realities of today, I rather expect to hear that people have started a petition to recall the governor of Alabama, if such a thing is possible under the laws of that state.

The governor of Alabama is discovering that there is nothing that people hold quite so dear as their wealth—their money and their possessions. Wealth even influences the way we read (or don't read) the Bible. People *leave* churches where they think money is talked about too much, despite the fact that Jesus talked about money quite a lot in the Gospels. In some churches, people stay away from worship at pledge campaign time (ours will be in November, by the way) because they don't want to hear sermons about giving money or announcements about pledging. And all of us are constantly under the temptation to serve *wealth* rather than *God*—Jesus said that it is *impossible* to serve *both*.

Jesus' point in so many places in the Gospels, of course, isn't just a question of giving up our money. It is a matter of trusting God completely. It is a matter of devoting ourselves to God's purpose. It is a matter of being willing to discard anything that constitutes an obstacle to our free and complete obedience to God. If money and possessions were frequently an obstacle to responding whole-heartedly and single-mindedly to God in *first-century Palestine*, with its few luxuries and conveniences and opportunities for leisure, how much greater is *our* difficulty in hearing Jesus' commands about money and possessions in *twenty-first-century America*, where talk shows make a big issue of returning to "Christian values" and then preach that, essentially, we are entitled to hold on to as much as we can grab in this earthly life.

One day, a man came to Jesus and asked what he needed to do in order to have eternal life. As much as such things could be quantified, the man was a very moral individual—he kept the Ten Commandments, he informed Jesus, and he must even have recognized that Jesus was in some respect endowed with the authority of God. He was, according to all the standards of law-keeping and piety, a good man, blameless in terms of the statutes, pure in all respects of personal behavior. But Jesus perceived that there was something that was preventing the man from being truly free to love and serve God—something that was standing in the way of what the law was really all about. We don't have to assume that the man's claim that he had kept the law was either untrue or immodest. He himself seems to have sensed that he was not perfect—that something was missing from his response to God. "'Good Teacher, what must I do to inherit eternal life? . . .

I have kept all [the commandments] since my youth.' Jesus, looking at him, loved him and said, 'You lack one thing; go, sell what you own, and give the money to the poor, and you will have treasure in heaven; then come, follow me'" (Mark 10:17b, 20b–21 NRSV). The quickness with which the man said that he had kept *all* the *commandments* suggests that he was *also* keeping a sort of *tally*—that he had mentally checked off the requirements so far as he knew them. Now, he wanted to be complete in his fulfilling of the law. But eternal life isn't a matter of legalisms, and God's favor isn't a prize for being able to add up enough points. Were salvation a matter of legal achievement, this man would have been a shoe-in. But it isn't. It's a matter of *faith*—utter reliance upon God and trust in God's faithfulness. And the man didn't really *have* faith, as it turned out—not faith in *God*, anyway. Jesus told him to cast all of his dependence upon God by selling what he had and giving the proceeds to the poor, and then following Jesus on his vagabond itinerary toward the cross. But the man couldn't imagine not having his wealth and his possessions to rely upon. And "[w]hen he heard this, he was shocked and went away grieving, for he had many possessions" (10:22 NRSV).

Long centuries before Jesus was approached by the rich man, another rich man, named Job, did not have a choice about giving up his possessions. He had kept all of the commandments of God—that was why he couldn't figure out why he was no longer wealthy, but had lost his children and his livestock and his servants. God had no legal complaint against him; he protested to his friends, who were trying to convince him that he must remedy some moral oversight to get back into God's good graces, but we are told in the book that even *God* acknowledged that Job was completely blameless. At one point, he was ready to argue with God as in a courtroom to prove his innocence and demand that God account for the misfortune that had befallen him and stripped him of wealth and possessions and family and even his health. To Job's credit, his faith in God was a faith in God's justice. His trust in God had been undergirded by his conviction that God would never abandon someone who was so devoted to leading a moral life. But where was God—the God of justice—hiding now, allowing all of these calamities to befall him? It was unfair, what was happening to him. It was wrong by any known standards of behavior, human or divine. Ultimately, the Bible tells us, Job learned that we must have faith in God in all circumstances, that we must trust God despite life's assault upon our human notions of what is good, even what is just. Ultimately, the Bible tells us, we must be willing not only to trust God *theoretically*, but to *live out* that trust, allowing our faith to be stripped of every support and comfort and insurance and hope that is not God himself.

I have known a few people whose lives seemed almost scripted from the pages of the book of Job—people who suffered one misfortune after another, not in any way their doing, people who suffered the death of one loved one after another, in almost sense-numbing frequency—who not only did not give up on God, but became more deeply devoted to God, who refused to become bitter or withdrawn or miserly or vengeful. They did not regard themselves as singled out for life's unfairness. They did not take out their disappointments on others. When, after losing much of what the world values and esteems, a person finds him- or herself still loved and forgiven by God—when all other sources and hopes of solace and delight have been stripped away—then, perhaps, one knows for the first time what faith in God truly is. African Americans have known such faith, the slave relying on God more genuinely than the master. I have sensed the same quiet reliance among Native Americans—the Navajo Christians whom I interviewed for my dissertation several years ago, and with whom I continued correspondence and conversations. I have seen it in the eyes and heard it in the song of skid-row worshipers at Fourth Presbyterian Church in Chicago, who had no earthly treasure to give up, and who knew that they were living, day by day, taking the bread that came their way, in total dependence upon God's grace. Meanwhile, the rest of us, living in what is both the richest and the most religious nation in the world, struggle to have faith—I mean faith in God rather than faith in the things God has lavished upon us, faith that would survive being stripped of reputation and political freedom and the nearness of family, of affluence. I won't insult your intelligence by promising that I could and would remain just as full of faith as Job, were such tragedies to invade *my* life.

It had always been assumed that wealth and prestige were assurance of God's favor, signs that the wealthy and prestigious were "in" with God. The disciples, who must already have been dismayed that the rich man went away from Jesus shocked and grieving, must indeed have been perplexed, as Mark reports, when Jesus said to them, "'How hard it will be for those who have wealth to enter the kingdom of God! . . . It is easier for a camel to go through the eye of a needle than for someone who is rich to enter the kingdom of God'" (10:23b, 25 NRSV). Jesus did not mean that wealth in itself keeps a person out of heaven, but that having *faith* in one's money and possessions does—and that it is difficult indeed for someone who has money and possessions not to put their faith in their *riches* rather than in *God*. But, still regarding wealth as a sign of God's approval, the disciples asked among themselves, "'Then who can be saved?'"—that is, if even the *rich* aren't assured of salvation, then who *could* be? And "Jesus looked at them and said, 'For mortals it is impossible, but not for God; for God all things are possible'" (10:26b–27 NRSV). Peter, perhaps remembering that the rich man had turned away from Jesus when he heard the requirement that he sell his possessions and give the proceeds to the poor and then follow Jesus, said, "'Look, we have left everything and followed you'" (10:28 NRSV). Even though they didn't always understand what Jesus was saying or doing, the disciples themselves were an example of stripped-down faith. They had lost their families, essentially—had walked away from them, even. They had lost their job security—had walked away from their nets and their tax offices, in fact. They had lost their homes—had walked away from them to sleep under the stars and in barns, perhaps, and trust that there would be food enough and clothing enough as they followed Jesus through the villages and over the hills and along the shoreline and wherever he might take them. They had no pension plans to look forward to in their retirement—not even Social Security. They had Jesus Christ, who pointed them toward God, who is good. Without having thought much about it, without having planned it, without having calculated it, without having reasoned it out after balancing the checkbook and consulting the stock quotations, they had faith. They had surrendered every other security in life and had followed Jesus.

Well, I salute the governor of Alabama, who, while some Christians in his state have been raising issues of church and state by holding vigils around a statue, has dared to break a political taboo and exposed the deeper issue of just how serious people are about putting faith into practice—faith that has no toeholds other than simple trust in God and God's command to care for those whom *God* cares for. It will be interesting to see which master ends up being served. For, of all the challenges to our faith, none is more dangerous than our wealth, our money and our possessions, and our *desire* for money and possessions.

> As [Jesus] was setting out on a journey, a man ran up and knelt before him, and asked him, "Good Teacher, what must I do to inherit eternal life?" Jesus said to him, "Why do you call me good? No one is good but God alone. You know the commandments: 'You shall not murder; You shall not commit adultery; You shall not steal; You shall not bear false witness; You shall not defraud; Honor your father and mother.'" He said to him, "Teacher, I have kept all these since my youth." Jesus, looking at him, loved him and said, "You lack one thing; go, sell what you own, and give the money to the poor, and you will have treasure in heaven; then come, follow me." (10:17–21 NRSV)

Faith in God is faith stripped of everything that is not dependence on God alone. But Jesus told the disciples that day of something amazing that happens when we give up all our other dependencies and follow him. "'Truly I tell you, there is no one who has left house or brothers or sisters or mother or father or children or fields, for my sake and for the sake of the good news, who will not receive a hundredfold now in this age—houses, brothers and sisters, mothers and children, and fields with persecutions—and in the age to come eternal life'" (10:29–30 NRSV).

Twenty-Ninth Sunday in Ordinary Time

First Presbyterian Church, Ponca City, Oklahoma
October 21, 2012

Job 38:1–7
Hebrews 5:1–10
Mark 10:35–45

"Faith"

MOST OF YOU ARE aware that I was in Seattle last weekend, visiting my younger daughter Beth, who has just started her first year of college at the University of Washington. The two thousand miles between us meant that it was the first time she has ever started a new school year when I was not present for her first day of class, but I very much wanted to spend time with her before many weeks had passed and see for myself her new environment and how she seems to be doing in this new experience. She seems, by the way, to be doing fine.

In my mind, as I walked around the campus with her, I was taken back to her first day of elementary school, a couple of years after we had moved from Dodge City, where Beth was born, to Reno. My wife and I were somewhat concerned about how she would take to first grade, partly because it was far different from her two-and-a-half-hour kindergarten, which was designed for learning by playing, and partly because the entire summer between kindergarten and first grade her older sister and brother tormented her with stories about how awful it was going to be. They managed to have her in tears every time they talked about first grade and its work, work, work, teachers that were slave-drivers, and hardly any time on the playground. They might even have told her that she couldn't go to the bathroom all day; I don't know. By the time her siblings had "prepared" her for her first day of class, she was scared to death. Well, needless to say, Beth quickly discovered that first grade was *not* the way sister and brother had told it. And Beth enjoyed it very much, looked forward to it each day, learned that she could trust her teacher, and became wisely *less* trusting of her siblings.

Today, Beth is probably the most daring of the three. But for a long time, Beth was not a pioneer. She was not eager to have new adventures, but preferred repeating things she had already experienced. She was cautious, fearful, even, of the unknown. A lot of us are like that. Very few of us are bold trailblazers. Most of us feel much more confident following in another's footsteps, knowing that someone else has been this way before and survived the experience, found out that it was not something to be afraid of, but to accept as a part of life. I remember almost a dozen years ago that as I approached the threatening boundary known as turning fifty, I took some comfort from the fact that others before me had passed through that mysterious veil, that great unknown. It was a surprise and irritation to me when an AARP application came in the mail several months before my fiftieth birthday, and when, about the same time, the cashier in a restaurant queried whether I might qualify for their "senior citizens' discount."

But what was most sobering about that fiftieth birthday was that it seemed to me to be a benchmark on the way toward *another* mysterious veil, an even *greater* unknown, the boundary that poses the *ultimate* threat to us—death. Columbus returned to Europe to tell about his experience. Lewis and Clark came back east and testified that the American West could be survived. But no one has come back from the grave—save one, of course. And it is because of his testimony that we are gathered here. It is because of his appearances to his friends after his crucifixion that people have been gathering in his name for two thousand years—not so much to hear a moment-by-moment account of his experience as to hear the good news that he *did* survive the grave—that despite all appearances at the moment of his death, God would not let his spirit and his goodness and his wisdom and his mercy come to an end and be all for naught, but indeed, his death was only a new beginning of people's personal experiences with Jesus the Christ, no longer bound by the constraints of time and place. And apostles remembered that Jesus had said things like assuring them that *they* would have a place with God after death *too*, that even a criminal who confessed faith in him before dying alongside of him would be with him in paradise, because of what was happening on Calvary that day. God, who creates life and *cherishes* what has *been* created, was in it. Jesus was willingly laying down his life in obedience to what he understood God's purpose for him to be. The effect of his sacrifice was that *others* could follow him *into* and *through* that dark abyss of ultimate unknown without fear, but confidently, trusting God, who declared way back at the beginning of creation that *death* is a part of *life*, that bodies made from dust will wear out and return to dust, but whose whole purpose for creation was for God to have a loving fellowship *with* the creation—and so why would God allow that purpose to be defeated when we take our last breath?

"Since, then, we have a great high priest who has passed through the heavens, Jesus, the Son of God, let us hold fast to our confession," wrote the author of Hebrews. "For we do not have a high priest who is unable to sympathize with our weaknesses, but we have one who in every respect has been tested as we are, yet without sin" (Heb 4:14–15 NRSV). Jesus' experience of death and resurrection is not irrelevant to mortals like you and me, just because Jesus is the Son of God. Jesus was a flesh-and-blood human being, like us—uniquely the Son of God, yes, but completely human, subject to physical limitations, susceptible to pain, vulnerable to injury, destined, as *every* human being is, for *death*, but destined *also*, according to *God's desire* for every human being, for life *beyond* death. And the only thing that could stand in the way of that—our own ungrateful rebellion against God—Jesus' willingness to suffer unjustly and die for others has *overcome*. The result is that Christ occupies now the seat of highest honor in the eyes of God. And all those who are united with Christ in purpose and trust—all of those who are united to him in *faith*—are promised that death is not something to fear, even for *us* who are subject to physical limitations, susceptible to pain, vulnerable to injury, destined, as every human being is, to die.

Hebrews speaks of all this in terms of Jesus being a great high priest—*the* great high priest. A priest is someone who has been selected to offer the people's gifts and sacrifices to God in order to pay for their wrongdoing—to atone for their sins. In Old Testament days, these were *blood* sacrifices—animals offered up on the altar; the blood, the evidence of life in the animal, was required. For someone to *live*, someone or something had to *die*. Blood had to be shed to make up for the wrongdoing that the human being had done, for God had a perfect right to take that person's life for his or her transgression of God's commands. It's not that the priests themselves were morally perfect. In fact, the first sacrifice they offered each day was a sacrifice for their *own* sins. One of the *qualifications* of a priest was to be aware of his own weakness. Only *so* could he sympathize with the people he represented, not sit in judgment over them. Only after he had acknowledged his own sin and offered a sacrifice to atone for his own wrongdoing was he in any position to take the offerings of *other* people in his hands and sacrifice them on the altar. Not that he treated sin lightly—far from it! His very job of shedding blood showed the great seriousness of sin. His entire life was to be a testimony to the importance of keeping the law. But, in fulfilling his task, the priest must be able to combine being *severe* toward *sin* with having *sympathy* for the *sinner*, especially the ignorant and the wayward, for whom the sacrifices had the greatest effect. Deliberate wrongdoing and willful disloyalty to God were another matter—for these things, no sacrifice of a goat or a pigeon could be adequate.

But even the *best* priest could only pass on to *God* what the people said and offered, and even the *best* priest could only pass on to the *people* what God said in the law and the prophets. The *Son of God*, Hebrews testifies, is the great high priest, who is *himself* the revelation of God, who is, *himself*, the essence of human weakness and suffering, who is, *himself*, the sacrifice that will once and for all atone for human sin, small or great. The Son of God does not just take our gifts and offer them to God in hope that they will soften God up when it comes to judging our unintentional slip-ups. The Son of God himself *is* our salvation, even for the most despicable, most notorious, most intentional sinner. And it all has to do with his obedient suffering and his obedient death. Now, says Hebrews, he is "the source of eternal salvation for all who obey him" (5:9b NRSV).

I am not about to stand up here and tell you that death really isn't so bad, that it's something even to look forward to. For one thing, you wouldn't believe me, because you know I haven't experienced it myself. For another thing, that would make the sacrifice of Jesus Christ on the cross for our salvation nothing special at all. For some people, death comes peacefully; it can be a blessed end to pain of body or torture of spirit. But death for many is an excruciating thing; one thing about being a minister, as being a physician or a nurse, is that you see a lot of people die—with quite a few people, the *process* of dying, and with some people, the very *moment* of death. Even when death is not a *physically* painful event, it is *emotionally* painful—the thought of being cut off from one's loved ones, the realization that our experience of the world, our home, has come to an end (in Christian belief, our spirit doesn't just keep sort of hovering around in the world). For Jesus on the cross, all of these things were true: the physical pain—*great* physical pain—*and* the emotional pain of being cut off, at a relatively young age, from family and from friends still robust and healthy, plus, in his case, the pain of humiliation of being branded a criminal, a blasphemer, a traitor. Hebrews tells us that the death of Jesus was in every way as real as ours will be. But the very *humanness* of Jesus is what made it so meaningful that *he* was the pioneer through the gates of heaven. The very *humanness* of Jesus, who is now the *risen Christ*, is what makes God's promise believable and sure that though *we* die, yet shall we live. "In the days of his flesh, Jesus offered up prayers and supplications, with loud cries and tears, to the one who was able to save him from death, and he was heard because of his reverent submission. Although he was a Son, he learned obedience through what he suffered; and having been made perfect"—that is, perfectly qualified for his role as high priest because his suffering made him so radically suited to deal with our human weakness and our human temptation that he now knows first-hand—"he became the source of eternal salvation for all who obey him" (5:7–9 NRSV).

Death is still no picnic. There is nothing pleasant about it. And a Christian cannot expect to be exempt from any of its pain. In fact, when a couple of his disciples rather gleefully skipped over the reality of death in their eager thought of being in a position of prestige and privilege in the kingdom of heaven, Jesus asked them if they were first ready to face *death*—and not just a peaceful death, but very likely the same sort of painful, humiliating, unjust death that he would soon experience in Jerusalem. "'You do not know what you are asking,'" Jesus said. "Are you able to drink the cup that I drink, or be baptized with the baptism that I am baptized with?'" (Mark 10:38 NRSV). "Are you ready to participate in my suffering?" he was asking. "Are you willing to be judged and executed for the crime of being faithful to God in a world that doesn't believe in God's justice, doesn't practice God's love, doesn't grant God's mercy? Are you ready to live your life totally for others, and perhaps pour out your life for my sake, make a sacrifice of your life so that *others* might know the truth of God's love and forgiveness and have *eternal* life in *this* world? Are you ready to be a perfect servant, following not your *own* desires and inclinations, but the will of *God*, whose purpose, perhaps, can only be achieved on the cross?" At least *one of those very disciples* who had asked for a seat of glory—James—is said to have been martyred a few years later by King Herod Agrippa; you see, the questions that Jesus asked are not just hypothetical. "Then Jesus said to them, 'The cup that I drink you will drink'" (10:39b NRSV). Our faith may well put us in the situation of having the cup handed to us. And only in *faith* can we drink it.

Faith is obediently walking into the unknown, trusting the testimony of someone else who has been there—ultimately, Jesus Christ. It may be the unknown of forgiving someone who has wronged us terribly. It may be the unknown of surrendering what we have and giving it to the poor. It may be the unknown of leaving home and those we hold dear to follow Christ into the dens of disease and the hovels of despair and the ghettos of injustice and untruth, even if it puts us at risk—our fortune, our reputation, our life. Jesus Christ, our Lord and our Master and our friend, has already passed through the boundary of the unknown, has endured every pain and fear, and has become our Savior. He has won our salvation—an unshakable place in the kingdom of heaven—for you and for me, *so that we can be free in this life* to follow where he leads—to live, and die, in faith.

Fortunately, Beth had not just the teasing of her sister and brother to go on as she finally took that first step into the first-grade classroom, terrified by all their mischievous misinformation, made up and off the point. She also had the words of her mother and father about what first grade would be like, spoken to her in love and assurance, and she finally trusted *our* testimony more than *theirs*. That's what parents are for, be they earthly parents or a heavenly parent. We couldn't tell her the details of what would be happening every moment in Miss Laxalt's class at Bud Beasley Elementary School; she would have to find that out for herself. But we knew the *purpose* of first grade, because *we* had been in first grade once *ourselves*. We once *passed through* first grade. Just think: our great high priest, Jesus, the Son of God, who in every respect has been tested as we are, has passed through the *heavens*! And he has become the source of eternal salvation for all who obey him in faith.

Thirtieth Sunday in Ordinary Time

Spanish Springs Presbyterian Church, Sparks, Nevada
October 29, 2000

Job 42:1–6, 10–17
Hebrews 7:23–28
Mark 10:46–52

"Lessons Over a Stale Biscuit"

HAROLD MCCLELLAND, MALE, AGE thirty-eight, Internet entrepreneur, found himself standing in the late autumn drizzle at the corner of Front and Yonge Streets, not knowing exactly how he had gotten there. Much of the day was a foggy memory, seemed like a lifetime ago. His dot-com start-up had been promising—had been touted in leading industry publications, was poised to go public with expectations of a rocketing share price. But then the stock market had decided that it was *glutted* with dot-coms that had never shown a profit, and as the new industry began to *sag*, it had pulled the high hopes for Hal's bold little enterprise down with it. It had all hinged on Internet ad revenues, and suddenly all the companies with which he'd been in intense conversation had lost interest—weren't even answering his telephone calls and emails. For the past few years, his world had been centered on his dream, and now his dream had all but vanished.

In the meantime, the dreams that had *already* come *true* had *also* vanished. As he was getting ready to drive in to work that morning in his six-month-old Lexus—everyone told him that he *had* to have one—his wife of twelve years announced that she was taking the children and going home to Kingston for a few days. She had to have some space, she said, some time to think, and it was obvious that he could not care for the children in her *absence*, since he wasn't paying much attention to them when she was *around*. Their marriage, she said, had become unimportant to him the past couple of years. He hardly knew she was there, she said. No, he had not been a poor provider. No, he had never been abusive. No, he had never been unfaithful. The problem was that he was totally consumed with his company and his big plans, and where did that leave her and the little kids? Well, not so little anymore—seven and nine—but it was all too much, she said. She didn't know *when* she would be back. She was taking unpaid leave from her job. She would call the school about the children. Maybe she would call *him*. Right now, she just needed to get away.

The city looked dismal in the darkling late afternoon. Pedestrians were huddled under umbrellas, except for Hal, who hadn't planned to be walking anywhere and so didn't come prepared for the weather. Maybe he had been heading for a bar. Maybe he had been heading for the athletic club. Whatever the plan was when he left the office suite he had optimistically rented in one of the bank buildings, he had forgotten it, or it was irrelevant as soon as it had formed in his mind. Maybe if he kept walking, he could remember. That, or he'd find himself on the shore of the lake, staring at the steely blue water. And then what?

A sea of umbrellas had gathered around him at the corner, waiting for the walk light so they could surge ahead to the train station across Front Street. The commuter rush had begun. Hal was carried along with the tide, but managed to break free from the silent crowd as he reached the curb, and he kept walking down Yonge Street, underneath the railroad tracks. Just as he reached the shelter of the underpass, there was a buzzing in his coat pocket. "Hello," he said as he held the mobile phone up to his ear. "Yes, this is Harold McClelland." It was the finance company about the car payment again. "I told you, I need a few more days, and I'll make it—" He had never gotten telephone calls like this until a month ago. Now they came frequently. But this time there was a difference. "Then come and get it," he said with a mixture of anger and resignation. He clicked off the device and thrust it back into his coat pocket.

He started walking again, emerged from the underpass and was exposed once more to the drizzle, and then found himself under the expressway, safe from the rain but still getting wet, as water dripped down through cracks from the roadway above. Something about government cutbacks for public works crossed his mind. He leaned against a concrete pillar, the noise of traffic overhead and alongside him dispersing his thoughts before they were quite formed. His mind did manage to retrieve images of his Lexus, his company, his wife, his children. Would the house be the next thing to go?

Some movement behind the next pillar ahead of him caught his eye— the only thing within sight that was moving and that wasn't on wheels. Just then, a truck hit a pothole in the street alongside of him, and he was suddenly drenched by a spray of gritty, oily water. He shouted out in surprise and disgust. He looked around himself and down at his feet, his arms outstretched, water dripping from his hair, unable to see through his glasses.

"Hey," came a voice from in front of him.

He lifted his head and wiped the dirty water from his face. He opened his eyes to a blurred image of short purple hair framing a face that featured some kind of green gemstone attached to the left side of the nose.

"I've got a fire," purple-hair said.

He shook the water from his glasses and wiped his eyes with the sleeve of his wet coat, and saw in front of him a girl—age seventeen or eighteen, he guessed—dressed in a long, dirty trench coat.

"Over there," she said, jerking her head toward an oil drum.

Hal had never thought before about what happened to the squeegee kids in the wintertime. Apparently, this one had set up a permanent address at the corner of Yonge Street and Lakeshore Boulevard. His memory drifted back to the dozens of times that he had waved them off when they darted out into the stopped traffic to perform the unwanted service of cleaning already-clean windshields, ne'er-do-wells in a booming economy where surely anyone who *wanted* a real job could *find* one. Parasites, he had thought, after the initial amusement had worn off.

"Come on," purple-hair said, "unless your limousine is due."

He followed her, without saying anything, to the oil drum, which had a little flame of fire in it and a mound of wood scraps and cardboard alongside it—probably rubbish gleaned from the nearby construction sites that dotted the city's lakefront. "It'll warm two as easily as one," said purple-hair. She held her hands out over the makeshift fireplace, rubbed them, and then extended the right one to Hal. "I'm Annie," she said.

Hal had somehow missed the punk scene—he did, after all, fit the description of a "computer nerd" at university—and had never warmed to strange hair and pierced noses. But he managed to recognize Annie's gestures as hospitality, and he held out his clammy hand to shake hers, weakly. "I'm Hal," he said, checking a reflex to reach inside his coat and draw out a business card.

"You live down here?" Annie asked, sitting down cross-legged beside the oil drum and nodding toward the apartment houses and condominium complexes perched on the harbor front across the boulevard.

"No," he said slowly, "I'm just out for a walk." He felt that he needed to apologize for intruding upon her squalid little territory.

She crinkled her nose at this. "Bay Street's the other way," she said, then chuckled at her reference to the city's financial district. "Want an apple?"

This caught Hal off guard. "I haven't any change," he stammered.

Annie looked up at him with a confused expression, then shook her head. "No, no. I mean, I'll *share* it with you." She reached into a cardboard box behind her and produced a scrawny bit of red fruit. "A reject from the green grocer over on Bathurst Street," she said, more in the way of explanation than apology.

"No, thank you," said Hal.

"Biscuit?" Annie tried again, pulling a round pastry from her coat pocket and holding it out for Hal's inspection.

Feeling guilty about the apple, he decided that the biscuit was the safer item, even though it had probably attracted lint and whatever else resided in the girl's pocket. He sat down on the grimy pavement. "Thanks, yes." He took it from her hand and bit into it gingerly, not knowing how hard it might be. It proved to be not as bad as he anticipated, though obviously days old.

"I've got some grape juice." She produced a little glass juice bottle that was about half-full of the purple liquid.

Hal wasn't ready for this degree of intimate germ sharing. "No, thanks. Maybe later."

"My work's a little slow now," said Annie, stretching out her legs and leaning back on her elbows. "Provisions are kind of low."

Hal smiled weakly. "My business is slow now, too," he said, then wondered what he was doing talking to a squeegee girl under the expressway on a rainy afternoon. She looked at him with a steady gaze inviting more of an explanation. "Well, why not?" he thought to himself. What harm could it do? "My company's on the rocks. My car's about to be repossessed. My wife left with the children this morning."

"That's rough," Annie said, still looking at him from her reclining position.

He expected her to say more in the way of sympathy at hearing how his entire universe had collapsed, but instead, she simply asked, "What went wrong?"

"I don't know," he said, and was surprised at the sound of the words. "I really don't know. I was doing everything by the book. Looked like we had a great future. Never cheated anybody. Thought I was doing everything I was supposed to—including at home." He shook his head. "It doesn't seem right." Then again, but more to himself this time, "It's just not right."

"Life's that way," said Annie, not at all cruelly.

"Why do you do this?" Hal asked her after a long silence, having managed to finish off the biscuit and wishing that he had taken up her offer of grape juice to help the last dry bit reach its destination.

"Do what?" she asked.

"Live like this." His words did not sound rude to him, but natural.

She shrugged. "Why not?"

"But shelter, a home, security, comfort, knowing where your next meal is coming from—"

"I've got what I need. I'm alive."

"Yes, but—" He couldn't think of anything else to say to someone who just didn't seem to understand what was so obvious to him. For her part, Annie did not seem the least bit offended. Then Hal blurted out, "Surely, you had dreams."

"Dreams? Yeah. There was Marty." Hal looked at her expecting an explanation. She said simply, "I don't know where he is now." She looked at him for a while and then said, "You get over it."

This was not the way Harold McClelland looked at life, and he felt a slight revulsion at Annie's casual acceptance of her social situation. He was a planner. He did his homework. He was honest. He was convinced that he had earned everything that he had ever achieved. He was one who believed that all things come to people who work hard, or at least work *smart*. But then, immediately, he remembered the painful new reality of his own situation—where planning and preparation and hard work had brought him. His face just then must have betrayed how the firm convictions of his existence had abruptly been yanked out from under him—the face of a person who has suddenly realized that he only *thought* he had it all figured out. Annie scooted closer and put her arm around him. His head yielded to her gentle pull, and he rested it on her shoulder as tears came to his eyes—a man twice her age being comforted by a girl with purple hair and a pierced nose. She didn't say anything. They just sat there.

After several minutes, Annie said, "You know, you're wrong about my not knowing where my next meal is coming from."

Hal drew away from her and looked at her questioningly.

"Come on, get up." She stood up and threw a couple of pieces of plywood into the fire and started walking north on Yonge Street, a woman with a mission. Hal scrambled to follow her. The drizzle had become a more steady rain. Hal wondered if her coat was going to be streaked with purple. She plunged across Front Street, swimming uptide against the commuters who were now streaming toward Union Station, and then turned left on the sidewalk toward the hulk of hotel that was one of the city's revered landmarks. Hal was several steps behind, trying to keep up through the crowd that was hustling to get somewhere dry. A turn down a dusky alleyway brought them to a loading dock—the delivery entrance, deserted of humanity and empty of promise, it seemed, except for a crate turned upside down just outside a steel door. Hal stood in the alley as Annie climbed the few concrete steps up to the crate, lifted it, and uncovered a Styrofoam container. She replaced the crate and descended the stairs to where Hal stood in the rain shadow of the tall building. Annie popped open the lid of the container to reveal a red pasty liquid covering some pale doughy-looking substance and some bits of meat. "Italian night," she said, smiling at Hal as she closed the lid back down on the container. "Looks like ravioli or tortellini and something Parmesan."

They started walking back toward the street. Annie explained, "Billy used to be in my line of work, but couldn't handle the stress." She laughed. "Got a job as a dishwasher. Now he sets out the leftovers from the first set of plates he gets back every night." As they emerged out onto the sidewalk and into the rain, Annie repositioned the Styrofoam container under her arm and ducked her head a bit. "May not know *what* dinner is, but I always know where it's coming *from*."

Hal looked at her with a budding admiration. Filtering out the hair and the pierced nostril, he noticed for the first time how pretty her face was.

"We'll eat well tonight," she said as they reached the corner of Yonge Street and turned back toward Annie's territory under the expressway.

Seeing a man with an umbrella and a mobile phone at his ear walking toward the train station, Hal remembered that he had turned his own cell phone off after the call from the finance company. They had probably given up trying to call him back by now, he thought, and he reached into his pocket and turned the device back on so that it could receive calls. Annie threw some damp cardboard into the oil drum, and then she and Hal again sat down on the pavement. Annie produced two plastic forks from her cardboard box and handed one to Hal.

"Could I have some of the grape juice now?" Hal asked.

Annie nodded and smiled, and reached back into the cardboard box for the bottle. Just then, the phone in Hal's pocket buzzed. "You go ahead and start," he said to Annie. "I'd better go where I can get better reception."

He stood up and walked over to the pillar he had been leaning against when he first spotted Annie, and held the little device up to his ear. "Hello," he said.

"Hal," said a voice at the other end of the line. "I've been trying to get you for over an hour." It was his partner, David Miller, his voice cutting in and out.

"Just a minute," Hal said, and he walked out from under the expressway and stood in the rain. "I can hear you better now."

"Why'd you turn your cell phone off? NuTech called just after you left the office. They want exclusive advertising rights on the site! They want to sign a contract tomorrow! We made it, Hal. We made it!"

"That's great," Hal said, his hand shaking and lips quivering, but his voice did not match the breathless exuberance at the other end of the conversation.

"What's wrong?" asked Dave. "This means everything!"

"It's great," Hal agreed, "but it's not everything." He glanced back at Annie's shadowed form, seated on the ground beside her oil drum.

"Well," said Dave, "with the roller coaster we've been on the past few weeks, you'll have to explain that one to me later. Oh, listen," he added. "Your wife called. She's been trying to get you. Said to tell you she'll be waiting for you at home with dinner. Something about turning around at Belleville. Does that make sense?"

This brought a smile to Hal's face much broader than the news about the contract with NuTech. "Thanks, Dave," he said. "I'll see you tomorrow." He returned the cell phone to his coat pocket and felt his car keys. Would there be anything in the parking stall to drive home in? he wondered. Oh well, he could take the subway to Victoria Park and walk home from there. It didn't matter that it was raining. He was already wet.

As he approached the oil drum, Hal saw that Annie had placed the Styrofoam container of Italian scrapings on the ground in front of her, but hadn't yet begun to eat. Her hands were clasped in her lap and her head was bent forward, her eyes closed. He very much wanted to tell her his news, but first he asked her, "Why aren't you eating? What are you doing?"

At first, she didn't answer. Then she looked up at him and said, "I'm saying grace."

All Saints' Day

First Presbyterian Church, Ponca City, Oklahoma
November 1, 2012

Isaiah 25:6–9
Revelation 21:1–6a
John 11:32–44

"Anticipation"

"For as often as you eat this bread and drink the cup, you proclaim the Lord's death until he comes" (1 Cor 11:26 NRSV). So Paul explained what happens at the eucharist, the sacrament of the Lord's Supper. Jesus, according to Paul, and according to Luke, had instructed his disciples, "Do this in remembrance of me" (11:24c NRSV; Luke 22:19c NRSV). And the command has been carved into the minds of countless worshipers as they have read those words Sunday after Sunday, chiseled into the communion tables and altars of their sanctuaries. Somehow, because we know that the words were spoken by Jesus at a specific time and place, now nearly twenty centuries ago on the night before the drama of Calvary, a lot of us suppose that to "Do this in remembrance of me" means to be aware of an historical event that happened long ago—Jesus' sacrifice on the cross, symbolized in bread broken and wine poured out.

But the meaning of "remember" here, as quoted by Paul and then by Luke, is more along the lines of keeping a person in mind presently. "Remembering" your friends at Thanksgiving, for instance, or at Christmas, or on their birthdays, with a phone call or a card or a present, is not retrieving an historical fact. It is maintaining a living relationship. It is appreciation for what that person means to you. It is honoring that person's significance in your life, and pledging the continuation of that significance and appreciation and relationship into the future. To gather at the Lord's table is not about honoring a dead hero, but renewing and keeping fresh and giving witness to our relationship with a living friend—one whose words and actions in fact shape us and affect us and challenge us and encourage us today to live in imitation of him, copying his kindness and his generosity and his mercy and his love, copying his obedience and his trust and his devotion and even his sacrifice.

Part of the reason for the decline of active Christianity in Western culture is the increasing inability of people to live in anticipation. Whatever else one may say about the powerful forces of advertising and immediate gratification, including instant communication and overnight shipping and all the other evidence of cultural impatience, Europe and North America and now a growing part of the rest of the world have become physically and psychologically intolerant of waiting. In a few weeks, your pastor will be engaged again in the annual battle of trying to help a congregation to focus on Advent, the Christian season of trustful patience. I will be asked why it is that we don't sing Christmas carols, why we don't hear the story of the manger, until Christmas Eve. And the questions and—let us be honest—complaints will demonstrate the very modern disinterest in what the Advent season asks of people of faith, of what the Advent season means: to live in hopeful expectation of a certainty that is not yet—Christ's return, and God's consummation of history. Advent is not a warm-up for Christmas. It is a looking forward to the conclusion of what *began* with the birth of Christ, what was *forecast* in his teaching, what was made *possible* in his crucifixion, what has been *guaranteed* in his resurrection. And all of that we *remember*, in the sense of recalling to mind and proclaiming its truth and doing something about it, whenever we come to the Lord's table.

Last February, I had the privilege of standing on the Mount of Olives and looking across the Kidron Valley at the city of Jerusalem, built on Mount Zion. Then I walked its streets. I felt, I saw, I heard, I smelled, I tasted the city bustling with people from many cultures, many backgrounds, many different religions. In Jewish theology, what is most important about Jerusalem is that it was the location of the temple of God—referred to repeatedly in the Old Testament as the place where God officially had communion with humankind. The temple is gone, of course, and the New Testament scriptures point to its replacement as the locus of communion between God and humankind with Jesus the Christ. *In* Christ, pure divinity meets genuine humanity. *Through* Christ, you and I best come to know God. What the Old Testament says about Mount Zion in concrete geographical terms, the New Testament asserts to be true of Christ himself. "On this mountain the Lord of hosts will make for all peoples a feast of rich food, a feast of well-aged wines, of rich food filled with marrow, of well-aged wines strained clear"

(Isa 25:6 NRSV). Of that future banquet, this table is the pledge. "And he will destroy on this mountain the shroud that is cast over all peoples, the sheet that is spread over all nations; he will swallow up death forever" (25:7 NRSV). Of that future hope, this table is the testimony. "Then the Lord God will wipe away the tears from all faces, and the disgrace of his people he will take away from all the earth, for the Lord has spoken" (25:8 NRSV). Of that future redemption, this table is the anticipation. "It will be said on that day, Lo, this is our God; we have waited for him, so that he might save us. This is the Lord for whom we have waited; let us be glad and rejoice in his salvation" (25:9 NRSV).

The Bible invites us over and over again to live *today* in the truth of what God summons us to *anticipate*. The God for whom all of history is as the blink of an eye calls on his faithful people to be so hopeful, to be so obedient, to be so trusting, that we allow neither clocks nor calendars to obscure our clear vision of everything that God has promised at history's end, and what the *prophets* proclaimed as true, though it was not yet. And so faithful people needed to live as if it were *already*, so *John* proclaimed as true in the Revelation: the holy city, the new Jerusalem, coming down out of heaven from God, prepared as a bride adorned for her husband. It will be the very experience of God dwelling among us, no longer distant in some faraway place, but within sight, within reach. And was it not in Jesus Christ that the Word of God became flesh and lived among us? We have already experienced the truth of what God has pledged will be: "See, the home of God is among mortals. He will dwell with them as their God; they will be his peoples, and God himself will be with them; he will wipe every tear from their eyes. Death will be no more; mourning and crying and pain will be no more, for the first things have passed away" (Rev 21:3b–4 NRSV). There will be a new Jerusalem, where, seated on his throne, no longer distant and unreachable in heaven but present in our midst, God will make all things new, and we will be forever in communion with God and with the Lamb. In that city of God, into which peoples of every nation are to be gathered— are we to remember Christ himself, and think of all that his church should be?—death simply ceases to be, along with sorrow and hurt and weeping. And it is a city—a place of many, vastly inclusive of multitudes, a community interdependent and forbearing, living side by side and sharing—not a cloistered bliss all constructed on satisfying selfish and competing desires and feeding materialistic and gluttonous appetites, but fulfilling God's own dream of community that prompted the very first acts of creation.

So what scripture promises is in no sense a rapturous escape from the world and all of its needs, but a grateful affirmation of God's creation and the satisfying of its purpose at the most profound level. The new Jerusalem is paradise restored, a safe and secure garden where human labor honors God's bounty and where human compassion mimics God's love. In fact, this paradise regained is simply full and absolute communion with God himself. "'It is done!'" God said to John. "'I am the Alpha and the Omega, the beginning and the end. To the thirsty I will give water as a gift from the spring of the water of life'" (21:6 NRSV). Isn't that the gift of Jesus himself, God's Son, offering freely for you and for me and for all people, bubbling up and refreshing and renewing and giving life eternal to all who enter the open gates? What God promises at the end of history, those who are in Christ Jesus already experience. What God pledges as the certain future, those who are in Christ Jesus are already tasting and drinking in at the familiar meal that is the foretaste of the great banquet to come.

We pray in anticipation. We worship in anticipation. We eat and drink in anticipation of the fullness of what we are already experiencing in the community of believers, of the new Jerusalem, which is already prefigured in the person of Jesus Christ, whom we know and trust and love and acknowledge as Lord and Savior. We dine in remembrance of Christ, testifying that the end of history is not an event, but a person, as we give witness that the end of our present life will not be a cataclysmic fall off some treacherous cliff, but the welcoming embrace of our truest friend. And the final judgment will not be the utter destruction of all that we have known, but the perfect transformation of all that God has made. And, trusting that, all of our present activity, all of our current relationships, must and shall be transformed. We live now in anticipation of what is yet to be, but knowing that what is yet to be must transform us today into Christlikeness.

And so it is that what we do at this table, we do in remembrance of him. In the closing words of Revelation and all of scripture: "The one who testifies to these things says, 'Surely I am coming soon.' Amen. Come, Lord Jesus" (22:20 NRSV)!

Thirty-first Sunday in Ordinary Time

Spanish Springs Presbyterian Church, Sparks, Nevada
November 2, 2003

Ruth 1:1–18
Hebrews 9:11–14
Mark 12:28–34

"Love Beyond the Law"

THERE IS A BASIC difference in the philosophy behind the law in most European countries from the philosophy upon which American jurisprudence is founded. Of course, we inherited the principles of common law from England, developed in actual cases over centuries of legal decisions, whereas most of Europe operates under legal codes that leave little to the discretion of the court. But beyond that, whereas in America our legal system is based upon the theory that we should not harm a person or his or her property and that we will face consequences if in fact we *do* commit harm, in Europe there is a more positive obligation to do the other person *good*. So, for instance, someone driving past a car accident in America has no legal obligation to stop and render assistance, but in most of Europe, as I understand it, it is illegal to pass someone by in such a situation without offering aid. So contrary to expectations is it in America to stop and render aid to an injured motorist or pedestrian or whatever that many states have had to pass "Good Samaritan" laws to protect aid-givers by granting immunity from lawsuits for damage they might cause while attempting to be helpful. In most of *Europe*, you would be in legal trouble if you didn't *try*. It seems that the American approach is that the law is much more about "Thou shalt not" than about "Thou shalt." That may have to do with perceptions of human nature. Do people need *restraining*, so that the law is something that is supposed to *keep* people from doing certain things? Or do people need *prompting*, so that the law is something that is supposed to encourage people to *do* certain things?

Jesus wasn't the first person to link love of God with love of neighbor. But it is interesting, I think, that he and a scribe, of all people, agreed on the priority of love as the greatest of all duties. The scribes were experts in the law—all of the intricacies, all of the requirements. The law was their life, so to speak. But one perceptive scribe agreed with Jesus that, in fact, if *love* were our overriding rule, we would naturally fulfill all of the *other* laws in the Bible. Jewish teachers were always looking for ways to summarize or prioritize all of the many laws that they regarded as binding. After all, they calculated that there were 613 commands in the scriptures—365 prohibitions ("Thou shalt not's") and 248 positive requirements ("Thou shalt's")—and it was all too much for most people to remember. So what the scribe was asking Jesus—which commandment is first of all?—was something that the scribes asked and debated among themselves, though some scholars held that there was no priority among the commandments, that they were all of equal importance. But Jesus said, "The first is, 'Hear O Israel: the Lord our God, the Lord is one; you shall love the Lord your God with all your heart, and with all your soul, and with all your mind, and with all your strength.' The second is this, 'You shall love your neighbor as yourself.' There is no other commandment greater than these" (Mark 12:29–31 NRSV). The scribe agreed. And Jesus said to him, "You are not far from the kingdom of God" (12:34b NRSV).

Now, that raises a question. If Jesus thought that the scribe had answered rightly, why did Jesus judge the man still to be outside the kingdom? I think it can only be that the man needed to *live* the priority of love that he *professed*—knowing *about* loving God, and knowing *about* loving neighbor, isn't the same as *loving* God, and certainly isn't the same as *loving* neighbor. Perhaps the man was better at *debating* the issue than *doing* what he knew to be *necessary*. Maybe he was good at telling *others* to stop and help the victim lying beside the road, but he *himself* always passed by on the other side.

Jesus understood love as something volitional—something that we can will and decide to do—and knew that it is something that is expressed in hundreds of everyday ways. But Jesus' own actions, his own deeds, are what give his commands to love God and neighbor their power—power that unsettles all legalism. He excluded any interpretation of the law that loses sight of God's will while seeking simply to observe all sorts of specific commandments—so he healed on the sabbath as well as other days, he permitted his disciples not to wash before dinner (a matter of ritual, not hygiene), he had no objection to their gleaning grain on the seventh day if they were hungry, he spoke to foreigners and ate with tax collectors. He loved beyond the law, knowing that the commandment to love is a command to do the *deeds* of love and to meet people's real needs, and that anything that stands in the way of such love has to collapse before it, because in that case the law is obstructing, not promoting, what the law was designed for in the first place.

One of the most beloved stories in the Old Testament is a case in point. One of the Ten Commandments—a positive "Thou shalt," and the only one of the Ten Commandments that includes a promise of good result—is this: "Honor your father and your mother, so that your days may be long in the land that the LORD your God is giving you" (Exod 20:12 NRSV). Exodus indicates that it was already well known among the Israelites even while they were still wandering in the Sinai, many years before they entered the promised land, many years before the time when the people of God were governed by judges, many years before they were ruled by kings. A woman named Naomi had gone from Bethlehem, the "House of Bread," with her husband and two sons into Moab in search of food. Now, much of the interest in the story has to do with the fact that people from Judah, where Bethlehem was located, had a deep dislike for people from Moab. It was rumored that the Moabites were descendants of the offspring of the incestuous relationship between Lot and his eldest daughter. The two countries had a long history of conflict and distrust, dating back to the wilderness wandering days. But famine makes such prejudices irrelevant; Naomi and her husband and sons did what they had to do. Once in Moab, however, Naomi's husband died. She was now a widow with two children in a foreign land. When her boys grew old enough, they naturally married women of Moab—something that would have been frowned on back home in Bethlehem. Then her sons died, leaving Naomi and her daughters-in-law, Orpah and Ruth, all without support, and in truly desperate straits. If Naomi had had other sons, it would have been their duty to marry the widowed daughters-in-law, but Naomi was now childless, and beyond the prospect of marriage and childbirth. So, when she heard that the famine had ended in Judah and that Bethlehem had become once again the "House of Bread," she determined at long last to return to her home. Her daughters-in-law started to accompany her, their mother-in-law, but she told them to return to their own mothers' houses in Moab. Orpah, after initially protesting, obeyed her mother-in-law's command.

But Ruth did not obey. She persisted in her intention to accompany Naomi back on her journey and to remain with her and care for her. "Do not press me to leave you"—the force of the Hebrew word makes it, "Do not press me to *abandon* you"—"or to turn back from following you! Where you go, I will go; where you lodge, I will lodge; your people shall be my people, and your God my God. Where you die, I will die—there will I be buried.

May the LORD do thus and so to me, and more as well, if even death parts me from you" (Ruth 1:16–17 NRSV)!

Ruth's response to Naomi's command is remarkable on a number of points. Her pledge of loyalty included giving up her own homeland and culture to go into what was certain to be a hostile social environment—the people of Judah hated the people of Moab. Maybe Naomi herself wasn't too happy to have Moabite women in the family, or to be the subject of the critical gossip that would surely befall her when she showed back up in Bethlehem with a Moabite daughter-in-law. She had apparently decided to live a miserable, bitter old woman the rest of her days, a victim of God's hand which had struck down her husband and her two sons. Some commentators suggest that she wanted no daughters-in-law around her as reminder of her tragic past, but a few verses after this morning's reading, she is quoted as saying to the people of Bethlehem that they should no longer call her "Naomi," which means "sweetness," but "Mara," which means "bitterness." In other words, all indications are that she fully intended to keep her tragic circumstances in front of her, and in front of everyone else, too. As the story turns out, Ruth ended up marrying a relative of Naomi's deceased husband, and bearing a son.

> Then the women said to Naomi, "Blessed be the LORD, who has not left you this day without next-of-kin; and may his name [that is, the name of the child] be renowned in Israel! He shall be to you a restorer of life and a nourisher of your old age; for your daughter-in-law who loves you, who is more to you than seven sons, has borne him." . . . They named [the child] Obed; he became the father of Jesse, [who was] the father of David (Ruth 4:14–15, 17b NRSV),

the greatest king of Israel.

"Honor your father and your mother" (Exod 20:12a NRSV), says the Fifth Commandment. Through the ages, that has been interpreted to mean, first and foremost, *obey* your father and your mother and older relatives in general, including father-in-law and mother-in-law. Orpah, Naomi's older daughter-in-law, did just that. After an initial protest, "she kissed her mother-in-law" and turned back to her own mother's house in Moab. "[B]ut Ruth clung to her" (Ruth 1:14b, c NRSV), as Ruth had once clung to her husband, now refusing to abandon Naomi even though it was her wish and her command. In other words, Orpah followed the law by obeying Naomi and leaving her. Ruth did *not* follow the law; because she *loved* Naomi, she did not *obey* Naomi, but refused to abandon her and became even indignant at Naomi's insistence.

But *Ruth* is the *star* of the story, and without this stubborn Moabite, this disobedient foreigner, there would have been no King David—a biological fact that has not escaped the notice of generations of Jews and Christians. As it turned out, Naomi was restored to "sweetness," her life was redeemed from "bitterness," through Ruth's disobedience of the law—Ruth, described by the women at the end of the book who were talking to Naomi as "your daughter-in-law who loves you" (Ruth 4:15b NRSV)—the daughter-in-law whose love was so profound, the daughter-in-law who was so loyal to Naomi and her need for support, that she was willing to give up everything of her own, even the god of her own people, even the common hope of eventually being buried in the soil of her native land. Ruth *loved* Naomi, was *loyal* to Naomi, *honored* Naomi, enough to go *beyond* the law, beyond *logic* even, to disobey the words of Naomi's mouth and, instead, fulfill the vows of her heart made on her wedding day. And God blessed Ruth's disobedience by making her the great-grandmother of Israel's great king.

The story of Ruth is not a prescription for how all mothers- and daughters-in-law are to relate to each other. But it is, I think, an instance of love of neighbor as *self* that gives substance to love of *God*, from which flow all the commandments, not as legalisms, but as promptings to faithfulness. "Honor your father and your mother" (Exod 20:12a NRSV). What Old Testament character did that more profoundly than Ruth, even as she stubbornly disobeyed her mother-in-law's orders, and thereby disobeyed the word of the law? "Remember the sabbath day and keep it holy" (20:8 NRSV). Who has ever done that more perfectly than Jesus, even as he healed the sick on the sabbath, fed the hungry on the sabbath, forgave sinners on the sabbath, and thereby disobeyed the word of the law?

> One of the scribes came near and . . . asked Jesus, "Which commandment is first of all?" Jesus answered, "The first is, 'Hear, O Israel: the Lord our God is one; you shall love the Lord your God with all your heart, and with all your soul, and with all your mind, and with all your strength.' The second is this, 'You shall love your neighbor as yourself.' There is no other commandment greater than these." Then the scribe said to him, "You are right, Teacher; you have truly said that 'he is one, and besides him there is no other'; and 'to love him with all the heart, and with all the understanding, and with all the strength,' and 'to love one's neighbor as oneself'—this is much more important than all whole burnt offerings and sacrifices." (Mark 12:28–33 NRSV)

God expects us not only not to do *harm* to others, but, in fact, to do *good* to them. The greatest commandment is to love—to love even beyond the law.

Thirty-Second Sunday in Ordinary Time

Spanish Springs Presbyterian Church, Sparks, Nevada
November 8, 2009

Ruth 3:1–5; 4:13–17
Hebrews 9:24–28
Mark 12:38–44

"Sacrificing"

IN ALL THE DISCUSSIONS of worship styles these days, all the comparison of "contemporary" and "traditional" and "alternative," the focus of whom it is that is being worshiped often gets lost. When the emphasis falls upon the *worshiper*—what he or she likes or doesn't like, what he or she is "getting out of it"—the fundamental question of *whether* and *how well* the God revealed in Jesus Christ is being honored, praised, thanked, and listened to seldom gets asked, and something really quite important is being ignored.

When the Bible speaks of "worship," it is referring to an event that is intentional, scriptural, and characterized by words and activities shaped by a tradition that itself has been shaped by reflection on who God is and what God deserves and what God wants of us. And, in much of the Bible, we can see that worship has to do with making an *offering* to God, and that the offering has the character of a *sacrifice*. The Old Testament speaks of sacrificial offerings being made at various shrines around the Holy Land, where the people gathered periodically to renew their covenant with God. Eventually, worship was centralized in the temple in Jerusalem, where sacrifices were made in atonement for sin. The writer of Hebrews explains that whereas the priests of old had to make *repeated* sacrifices, Christ made a sacrifice of himself on the cross, which was sufficient to atone for sins *once for all*, and so the sacrificial atonement that the priests made in the temple, which was itself destroyed three or four decades after Jesus' crucifixion and then was never rebuilt, became superfluous. But the notion of sacrifice has remained important in Christian thinking and continues, or *should* continue, to influence our understanding of worship and what it means to live faithfully. Specifically, the biblical emphasis on sacrifice should prompt us to consider what it means to make an offering that is acceptable to God and not to take our salvation for granted.

As the time of the Passover was drawing near, Jesus was teaching in the temple, where sacrifices were still being made upon the great altars and where various religious officials were engaged in their ritualistic duties and other activities. Some of the religious officials, at least, seemed to be making quite a display of their status, perhaps wearing their elaborate festal garments even though it was not a high feast day, relishing the deference being shown them by religious underlings and by the public at large, waiting even to be greeted in public places before they would return the greeting, much as a lower-grade soldier is expected to salute a higher-ranking officer before the officer returns the salute. There must have been some scribes present who were parading their piety to be seen and admired by others, eager to have a wider audience than simply God for their prayers, preening their souls for the approval and acclaim of whoever might notice. "As [Jesus] taught, he said, 'Beware of the scribes, who like to walk around in long robes, and to be greeted with respect in the marketplaces, and to have the best seats in the synagogues and places of honor at banquets! They devour widows' houses and for the sake of appearance say long prayers. They will receive the greater condemnation'" (Mark 12:38–40 NRSV).

Whether the reference to widows' houses means that they were sometimes designated as trustees or executors of the estates of men who had died and then turned their wives out of the dead husbands' homes, we don't know. In that case, they probably compensated themselves handsomely for the services they were performing for the estate. In ancient Israel, widows did not inherit their husband's property; a woman whose husband had died had to rely upon the generosity of her family or upon what little public assistance there was in ancient Palestine—unless, of course, some other man took her for his wife. A lot of widows had to turn to whatever they could to make money to live on, and not a few of them became prostitutes. The special concern of the Old Testament prophets that widows be cared for properly was an acknowledgment that they usually had to live a hand-to-mouth existence.

Perhaps Jesus' statement here about the scribes and widows' houses simply means that the scribes didn't mind oppressing widows and other poor people in the *morning* and then expected to be admired for their ostentatiously pious prayers to God in the *afternoon*. At any rate, in the very next scene, still in the temple, Jesus sat down where he could see the large trumpet-shaped metal containers, thirteen in number, where people entering and leaving the building made monetary offerings for the temple. "Many rich people put in large sums" (12:41b NRSV). You could tell, if you had been there, because of the noise a bunch of coins would make as they were tossed into the receptacles. Do you remember how heads used to turn in casinos whenever a slot machine poured out a mound of coins into the metal tray, and everyone could hear the telltale noise of metal on metal even without all of the newer electronic sound effects? Maybe whoever designed the temple treasury had the same understanding of human psychology that slot-machine manufacturers have. Surely the noise of a large number of coins being tossed in the containers would get a lot of people's attention, and they would naturally be curious who had made an offering of so much money.

On this occasion, just after warning against the ways of the scribes who made an exhibition of their religion and "devoured widows' houses," Jesus noticed that many rich people were depositing a lot of coins. Then a poor widow came along and dropped in two small copper coins which together made a penny, perhaps the price of a loaf of bread. Jesus was impressed. He called his disciples and drew their attention to the woman's deed. "Truly I tell you, this poor widow has put in more than all those who are contributing to the treasury. For all of *them* have contributed out of their *abundance*; but *she* out of her *poverty* has put in everything she had, all she had to live on" (12:43b–44 NRSV). Though only a tiny *fraction* of what the *wealthy* contributed, *hers* was the *greater* offering, for *it* was a *sacrifice*. Large as it was in amount, what the *others* had contributed they would not even *miss* at the end of the day. It wouldn't jeopardize their house payment or car payment. It wouldn't keep their children out of Harvard. It might even provide a useful tax deduction. It didn't hurt at all, and required hardly any faith in God's promise to provide for tomorrow. But the *widow* made a *sacrifice*. She had so *little*—only enough to last her through the next meal—and *that* she had given *away*, trusting God to care for her future needs somehow, and thankful that God had cared for her needs in the past and the present, making an offering from her heart.

We are not told how the disciples reacted. Were they positively impressed, as Jesus was? Did they praise God for the woman's faith? Or did they think, when they heard she had given everything she had, that the widow had committed a very foolish act indeed—inconceivable, totally irresponsible? Did they even understand the point Jesus was making?—that the gift that *counts*, whether it's a gift to God or a gift to a family member or a gift to a friend, is the gift that *costs*. A gift that costs us nothing, has no real effect on what and how we spend on *other* things, has made no demands on our time, has required no alteration of our plans, is a gift that really doesn't *mean* much. Jesus didn't denounce the offerings that people were making out of their abundance, out of their surplus beyond what they needed to live their lives of affluence and comfort. He had wealthy friends, and eventually the ministry of Jesus' apostles would benefit from wealthy patrons. But Jesus taught that the *sincerity* of a gift is to be measured not simply by the *size* of the gift, but against what is *left* after the gift is *made*. The *sincerity* of a gift is to be gauged by whether it constitutes a *sacrifice*. Of all the contributors Jesus saw tossing money into the treasury, only the poor widow made a *sacrifice*. *She* put in her next *meal*. *Hers* was a gift from the *heart*. And the Son of God took notice.

In comments about the war effort in Iraq and Afghanistan and the fact that life for most Americans has been relatively unaffected, several people inside and outside of Washington, both those who agree with the war and those who don't, have lamented over the past few years that the nation as a whole has not been asked to make a sacrifice. During World War II, our nation's leaders fostered a belief that success required a common effort and demanded sacrifices from every household. But our leaders today have never called on the average citizen to give up anything of significant monetary value to fight what has been called "the war on terror"—no tire rationing, no sugar rationing, certainly no gas rationing; indeed, we were at first encouraged to keep on *spending*. Once upon a time, the call to sacrifice was noble. When President Carter issued it during the Arab oil embargo, he was ridiculed. In a consumerist and materialistic culture, in which the economy is no longer based on the purchase of *necessities* but of conveniences and gadgets and amusements, the habits of instant gratification so methodically drummed into us have become deeply ingrained. For an entire generation, the notion of sacrifice is not only *alien*, it is *unthinkable*. No wonder so many megachurches have chosen not to put up a cross. No wonder some people balk when they hear the word "pledge."

But here in the very last episode in Jesus' public ministry before he was arrested and tried and crucified, Jesus talks about the importance of giving until it hurts. And by that, he clearly didn't mean living with one less latte each week, as is sometimes humorously said around stewardship time. He was talking about making a *sacrifice*, doing *without* in a way that one would *notice*, and trusting that God would provide for the things that were really necessary. The scribes, who liked attention, probably made ostentatious gifts that altered their lifestyles not the *least* as they went on their way to evict widows from their houses. But the widow, who most likely no longer had a house of her own, voluntarily gave up even the certainty of her next meal as an offering to the God who, she knew, had provided every meal she had ever eaten.

How many of us have ever really made a sacrifice for God, or for Christ's church? I am very sure that all of us have given out of our abundance, and those gifts have been important, without question. But how many of us have ever chosen between giving to God and buying even the simplest meal? And if we *have* made that choice, was it based on our *faith* that God would provide in the *future*, or out of *fear* that God would *not*? Some few of us are facing real hardship—loss of job or other circumstance that raises questions about being able to remain in our home, drawing on already scant savings to pay utility bills, putting off medical treatment because of other expenses. But most of us have probably accommodated our giving to God in a way that we scarcely notice it, and certainly don't feel it as a sacrifice—nothing approaching the case of the poor widow who, letting go of self and every worldly security, committed completely to God's mercy. Jesus didn't just call the attention of the *Twelve* to her deed of faith. He called the attention of the *church* to it, offering her as an example to you and to me, asking, as he was about to sacrifice his life for our salvation—a gift of everything he had—what sacrifice *we* are willing to make for the *gospel*.

Thirty-Third Sunday in Ordinary Time

First Presbyterian Church, Dodge City, Kansas
November 16, 1997

1 Samuel 1:4–20
Hebrews 10:11–25
Mark 12:41—13:8

"What Impresses You?"

AN EPISCOPAL LAY MINISTER named Garret Keizer has written of his experiences in a small church in Vermont. One of the episodes in his book tells of the Saturday night Easter vigil service at which only two other people had come to worship. The great Easter vigil began with his lighting the Paschal candle and his prayer, "O God . . . grant in this Paschal feast we may so burn with heavenly desires, that with pure minds we may attain to the festival of everlasting light."[1] As he looked up after the prayer, he was struck by the miracle—or was it absurdity?—of three people gathered in a church on a Saturday night, with most of the rest of the world, and perhaps even most of the rest of the congregation, little concerned or even aware that a tiny group of faithful worshipers were hailing the greatest miracle of salvation that has ever been worked, offering their humble thanks to God for keeping his gracious promise to raise Christ Jesus from the dead and to open for us the gates of eternal life. Keizer described it this way:

> The candle sputters in the half darkness, like a voice too embarrassed or overwhelmed to proclaim the news: "Christ is risen." But it catches fire, and there we are, three people and a flickering light—in an old church, on a Saturday evening. . . . The moment is filled with the ambiguities of all such quiet observances among few people, in the midst of an oblivious population in a radically

---

1. Keizer, *Dresser of Sycamore Trees*, 73.

secular age. The act is so ambiguous because its terms are so extreme; [either] the Lord is with us, or we are pathetic fools.[2]

I have sometimes felt that way, ministering in the materialistic, technological, secular culture in which Christians find themselves today. I mean, the Christian faith is a *counterbalance* to culture rather than a *blessing* of culture. Indeed, either the Lord is with us, or we are pathetic fools. Several years ago, at the first Ascension Day service I ever led, for instance, three faithful joined the associate pastor and the organist and me. It was clearly a countercultural event, radical in the extreme, our gathering together to hear again *about* and give thanks to God *for* Jesus' being raised up into heaven to rule at the right hand of God the Father Almighty. But of course the gathering of six of us for Ascension Day was only a difference in degree from the radical countercultural event of setting aside time on Sunday from working and from golfing and from traveling and from sleeping in and from reading the newspaper and from whatever else, to give thanks to God, who made us and feeds us and shelters us and promises that death will not be the end of us.

Whenever Christians become impressed by and get comfortable with and take their cues from the ways of the culture around them, their lives can hardly serve as a heavenly critique of worldly values. Whenever Christian worship adopts the forms of the entertainment culture or the standards of the economy, it can hardly serve to turn people's hearts and minds toward the sober truths of God. Whenever Christian hopes rise no higher than the consumerist hype of the moment, they can hardly sustain us through the real crises of life. But simple things like devotion and forgiveness and generosity and trust are rather unspectacular in the eyes of the media that wants to shape our lives, that tells us in so many effective ways what we are *supposed* to regard as important and worthwhile. It will not even merit a footnote in the history books that, while the stock market was rocketing skyward or nosediving downward, while the nations were rattling swords over bent pride and broken promises, while politicians were being indicted and celebrities were being pursued, three people were gathered in a Vermont chapel defying the terror of death with a song of praise around the feeble light of a single sputtering candle, or that half a dozen people were gathered in a Kansas sanctuary to proclaim that there is a powerful truth that now rules in majesty above headlines and hormones. It's just not very impressive by the standards of today's movers and shakers, publicists and promoters.

Jesus and his disciples were at the temple one day. Perceptive as always, Jesus happened to notice something that probably no one else in the temple

---

2. Keizer, *Dresser of Sycamore Trees*, 73.

paid any attention to: a poor widow, faithfully putting two copper coins—only enough to make a penny—into the temple offering. Many rich people were putting in large sums; you could hear the thunderous clatter of metal on metal throughout the courtyard when they made their big contributions. Jesus pointed out the poor widow making her little offering that was all that she had, but the disciples were apparently unimpressed and said nothing. But as they came out of the temple—these country folk from Galilee, who had come up to the big city of Jerusalem with its huge ornate palace and its huge ornate temple and its huge imposing walls and its huge markets with crowds that tumbled out onto the streets—one of the disciples said to Jesus, "'Look, Teacher, what large stones and what large buildings!' Then Jesus asked him, 'Do you see these great buildings? Not one stone will be left here upon another; all will be thrown down'" (Mark 13:1b-2 NRSV). And Jesus went on to tell them that the things that get the attention of the world—the wars, the natural disasters, the famines—would be many before history would finally come to an end. In and of themselves, these catastrophes were unremarkable—the stuff of history books, perhaps, but only the *beginning* of the inexorable tide that would *one* day crash on the shore of creation's destiny. None of them was climactic. None of them was important enough in itself to assume that it marked the end of the world. They were minor sideshows in comparison with *God's* intentions for creation. And not even the greatest achievements of human ingenuity—indeed, not even the grand and glorious temple of Herod—would endure to the end. Only God's redeeming purpose, revealed in such unimpressive and overlooked deeds of faith as a poor widow putting all she had into the offering plate, or the soft glow of a candle dancing across the faces of a handful of worshipers gathered to hear the good news of the empty tomb and the lordship of Christ.

What impresses you? Grand and beautiful sanctuaries? You're in good company—that is what impressed the disciples as they were leaving the temple in Jerusalem. Multinationals, superstores, even megachurches? The bigger, our culture seems to believe, the better. Money? Fame? Whatever is new? We can spend a lifetime making money and missing life's genuine riches. Fame is not a very stable commodity in a civilization as fickle as ours. And whatever is new today is old tomorrow; what a waste. Perhaps it's miracles, as if someone *could* even tear down the temple and raise it up again in three days. And yet, what obviously intrigued Jesus about the temple was the simple devotion of a poor widow who gave 100 percent of the little she had in a gesture of faith. The movie theater or video store has much better special effects than even the megachurches can manage—cars and buildings and airplanes blowing up, whole cities even. Television is much faster paced—no awkward periods of silence when we are left to think our own thoughts or offer our own prayers. The golf course may have its frustrations, but at least our golf buddies don't expect us to sing, and figuring a scorecard seems much less threatening than filling out a pledge card. And the newspaper always has something new to get our attention, even if it is only different names and different places, whereas the gospel just keeps replaying the same old story of God's salvation.

We in the church today don't have the high drama of the sacrifices of old, when the priest would slaughter the animal brought by a sinner to make a blood offering as atonement. The knife raised, the lamb bleating, life, then death, then blood, the symbol of life, repeated time and time again to make up for the endless round of new sins. We do, occasionally, have a baptism, but we are tempted to think of this sacrament of dying and rising with Christ as cute and sentimental, rather than dramatic and life-shaping. The writer of Hebrews reminds us that the cycle of sin and sacrifice, sin and sacrifice, has been broken by God's own sacrifice of Jesus his Son for our sins. The sacrifices of old, dramatic though they were, were ultimately futile. They could never take away sin. They were spectacular shows, well intentioned, but finally unimportant in the light of *God's* intentions for creation. Still, they were much more impressive, really, than a man judged guilty and made to dangle on a cross amidst other criminals dangling on crosses. Surrounded by marble and gold, the priests were busy offering sacrifices for the hundreds and thousands of people who had come to the huge ornate temple for the great high feast of Passover, a lamb or a goat or a pigeon purchased for money, animal blood shed for human sin and the greasy smoke of the altars rising in great billowing clouds to heaven. Out there somewhere on the outskirts of town, amidst sweat and flies and moans, God was making his own sacrifice of what was most dear to him, and hardly anyone noticed or cared. By worldly standards, not very spectacular, not very unique, not very impressive. But enough to make those few words that we say every time we worship, and sometimes almost dance over automatically in our haste, whether it be three of us or three hundred, the most important words that we will ever say and that should impress us more than any other truth we can speak: "In Jesus Christ, we are forgiven." Forgiven through a sacrifice that *we* did not *make* and that *no one* can *repeat*. Forgiven of sins that by human reckoning may be trivial or may be egregious. Forgiven not by our own accomplishment but as a gracious gift. Doesn't that impress us enough to make worship of God the most important thing that we can do? Doesn't that impress us enough to make doing God's will the most joyful duty that we have? Doesn't that impress us enough to marvel at every miracle of a prayer whispered for someone in need, an hour spent in ministering to the hungry and the sick, a penny offered by someone who has few coins but much faith?

In the days, the years, perhaps the centuries to come, there will be impostors who hold themselves up as some sort of messiah or other. There will be wars and rumors of wars. Nation will rise against nation, and kingdom against kingdom. There will be earthquakes in various places, there will be famines. *They* will make the headlines. *They* will cause the comment. *They* will prompt the decrees. *They* will be the things that get the world's attention. There will be taller and taller buildings, bigger and bigger superstores, higher and higher stock prices, grosser and grosser movies, all for the purpose of trying to impress us for a moment or two before the next building comes along or the next superstore or the next market high or the next entertainment blockbuster of disgustingly poor taste. And there will also be widows putting all the tiny offering they can make into offering plates, and a few people going out of their way to do a deed of kindness and expecting and wanting nothing in return, a few people visiting the sick and the lonely and the bereaved, a few people standing *by* the shunned and the despised and the ridiculed. And there will be gatherings of people on Sunday mornings when they could be doing a hundred other things and on dark nights when no one else seems to care, lighting candles hopefully and defiantly and giving thanks to God for the truth of the words, "In Jesus Christ, we are forgiven," knowing either that the Lord is with them or that they are pathetic fools. We know which of these things will impress the *world*. What impresses *you*?

Evening before the National Day of Thanksgiving

Spanish Springs Presbyterian Church, Sparks, Nevada
November 26, 2009

Joel 2:21–17
1 Timothy 2:1–7
Matthew 6:25–33

"The Most Difficult Commandment"

SUMMER AFTER SUMMER IN my youth, I boarded a long yellow train and went to Kansas to visit grandmothers, uncles, aunts, and cousins. It frequently worked out so that it was right around harvest time, and the train would pass the endless golden fields of grain, some of them with combines already plunging into them. And along the way, the Portland Rose would speed past a hundred white concrete giants linked by ribbons of steel stretching from horizon to horizon. Soon they would all be filled with wheat, and then thousands of box cars and gondolas would carry Kansas's bounty to the mills and the bakeries to feed a large proportion of the world. Not every field would produce a crop every year, of course. There might be *too much rain*. There might be *too little*. There might be *enough* but not at the right *time*. There might be *hail* at precisely the *wrong* time. But those towering white giants were testimony to the fact that this was a productive land, a land of plenty, a land of such abundance that there was more than enough to supply every table in the nation and beyond, if it was *shared*. And the abundance, despite occasional years of drought or monsoon, could be relied upon.

In the 1960s, my grandmother and her husband, living near Delphos, were wheat farmers. My cousins at Manchester were farmers, and had most of their land in wheat. My uncle in Manhattan taught milling at Kansas State University. And many of the women in my family who lived in Kansas were superb bakers. So my annual trip on the Union Pacific to visit the relatives, almost from the time I stepped from the railroad platform onto the passenger car in Denver, was a journey into what Kansas was all about. But it was also an education in the marvelous and dependable providence of God. And I was able to relive those days, after a fashion, when, living in Dodge City, I took Jesse out to a church member's farm a few times and I helped Jesse up into the cab of the combine—they have cabs now, air-conditioned cabs, air-conditioned cabs with two-way radios and CD players—to take two or three swaths with the farmer.

Ours has always been a productive land, located in a temperate climate between two oceans, and the technology developed here to coax fruit and grain from the soil has been adapted to make many another land productive as well. But of course, it is not only our technology, not only our ingenuity, not only our toil that brings the grain from seed to maturity. More than anything *we* do, it is the seed itself, and the soil, and the rain, and the sunshine that bring about the annual bounty—gifts of a gracious and provident Creator for beloved and dependent creatures. And the fact that we can sow and reap what we sow, and that it is suitable to nourish our bodies, only points from the cultivated fields to the wondrous cycle of nature itself, which miraculously blossoms forth each spring and comes to climax each summer and autumn at God's gentle bidding.

So many places in scripture, God has promised to care for *creation*, and to care for *us*. So many times in our experience, we have witnessed the dependability of God's promises. So many days on the calendar have gone by that we do not take to heart the magnitude of God's blessings upon us and give thanks for them. We either take them for granted or, just as bad and perhaps even worse, we do not live our lives in trust that God will *continue* to bless us by honoring the promises tomorrow and the next day and the day after that. When has God failed to provide abundantly for humankind? For hundreds of years, the ancient Israelites held harvest celebrations to give thanks to God for a repeat performance of the earth's abundant yield, and now we Americans have enshrined thanksgiving for the Lord's perennial bounty of the field in our civic agenda. Some of us even remember that it is a time not merely for friends and family and feast and football, but first and foremost for worshiping God. But in spite of God's constant demonstration of the dependability of nature's cycle, which meets our most genuine physical need, and even the annual reminder of it on our calendar, many of us return shortly afterward to worrying whether the great elevators will be full *next* year, whether God will provide for our needs *tomorrow*. And God must wonder what *more* it takes to convince us that the divine promise is trustworthy.

Anxiety not only robs us of the joy of living that God intends for us. Anxiety is a direct disobedience of our Lord's command. Have you ever noticed, in the Sermon on the Mount, that Jesus did not say, "*You don't have to* worry," but "*Do not worry* about your life" (Matt 6:25a NRSV)? Jesus had just been teaching that we should not store up treasures on earth, but rather that we should concern ourselves with the reputation we are making for faithfulness in the eyes of God, and that a concern for wealth—which is an overabundance beyond what we actually need—means that we will be inattentive to God. "For where your treasure is," Jesus said, "there your heart will be also. . . . You cannot serve God and wealth" (6:21, 24b NRSV). Then he told the people gathered there on the hillside—many of them poor, some of them despised, if it was a crowd like the others that gathered to hear him teach—not to worry about the needful things of life—about food, about drink, about clothing. How remarkable of Jesus, or how remarkably insensitive! So many people there had nothing like a savings account, had no storehouses, had no annuities. And yet they were *there*—they *did* get along in life, somehow, without the security of savings accounts and storehouses and annuities. Any middle-class folks in the crowd who were perceptive enough to discern the truth of Jesus' words about birds of the air in the example of their poorer *neighbors* perhaps began to ponder their own inordinate interest in worldly security. Did the savings accounts and storehouses and annuities of the moderately affluent really render them any less anxious about life than their indigent neighbors in their poverty? Were their indigent neighbors who received their daily bread a slice at a time nourished any *less* than the *affluent* who kept extra loaves stored in the cupboard? If our minds were all set on the things of *God, no one* would lack the needful things of this earth. And if our hearts were all tuned to faith in God and in the provident care that God has shown repeatedly over eons of time, no one, regardless of station in life, would ever have reason to be anxious.

But anxiety sells. And because it sells, it is particularly acute in our age of consumerism and demagoguery. A large segment of the advertising industry was founded on the strategy of *creating* anxiety—how will you survive without a particular product, or what if your neighbors all have it and you don't? Every other year, we have a great biennial exercise in manufacturing social anxiety for political purpose—each successive election campaign seems to achieve new heights (or depths) of the art. The anxiety leads to greed, and the greed leads to depriving *some* people of their God-intended share in the bounty of the earth. But isn't it peculiar that the anxiety doesn't get any *less* as we accumulate *more*? In fact, it creates *greater* anxiety—*more* is never *enough*. We must have more *yet* to feel really secure. And when that more *doesn't* produce security, the answer is still *more*. What if there is plague? What if there is famine? What if medical costs skyrocket even higher? What if inflation reignites? What if the market crashes again? What if . . . ? What if . . . ?

"God helps those who help themselves," we piously remind ourselves and others, quoting as scripture something that the Bible nowhere says, and declaring in reality that if we help ourselves *enough*, it will become *irrelevant* whether God helps us or not. And we forget or ignore what the Bible *does* say: "You shall eat in plenty and be satisfied, and praise the name of the Lord your God, who has dealt wondrously with you" (Joel 2:26a–b NRSV). Which manner of behavior is based on faith in God—the feverish construction of storehouses and spending all of our todays in anxiety about having enough for our tomorrows, or the expectation of blessings of daily bread from a heavenly hand that has never failed us? Which practice is more likely to cultivate a habit of thanksgiving? And can we expand our thankful recognition of God's unfailing care beyond the tangible blessings of food and clothing and shelter, to engender within us a thankful recognition of God's unfailing salvation in Jesus Christ? A few years ago, North American radio audiences were charmed by NPR's and the CBC's playing of and telling the story behind a recording of a homeless man's simple repetitive hymn, "Jesus' love never failed me, Jesus' love never failed me, Jesus' love never failed me yet." Beyond every evidence that nature demonstrates God's unfailing and ample care for us stands the most convincing evidence that God offered in the life, death, and resurrection of Jesus Christ. How can we be anxious about tomorrow, whether it be *this* side of the grave or the *other*?

For most of us, the Lord's commandment not to worry about our life, what we will eat or what we will drink, or about our body, what we will wear, but instead to strive first for the kingdom of God and righteousness, may be the most difficult commandment of all. Perhaps because it is not couched in the language of "Thou shalt" or "Thou shalt not," we may not even have recognized it as a commandment. But Jesus was as serious about having only one God and trusting him that day on a mountain in Palestine as God had been about having only one God and trusting him that day on a mountain in Sinai. Partial faith makes for a divided heart. And thanksgiving to God cannot be genuine if our minds are ruled by anxieties. It flies in the face of common practice and conventional wisdom. It contradicts what is pounded into our psyche daily by Hollywood and by Madison Avenue. It is certainly not the way to luxurious wealth, but Christ assures us that neither is it the way to dismal starvation.

God knows our needs. God is *greater* than our needs. God will *supply* our needs, just as God has supplied our needs all our life long. When has the sun not risen? When has the earth not yielded some harvest? When has God ever cut us off from his all-sufficient love and care? Even the homeless and the hungry know that it is not *God* who has failed to provide, but greed springing from anxiety that rations what God has graciously provided for all his creatures in abundance. The way to live in faith, and the way to live faithfully, is not to be worried about tomorrow, but to be grateful for what God has done today. Only if we consciously see ourselves as dependent upon God as are the birds of the air and the lilies of the field, and live our lives accordingly, can we ever be free from anxiety, can we ever be truly thankful, can we, and our neighbor, ever fully enjoy what God has dependably provided for all.

Yet once again *this* year, the blade has emerged from the soil, and then the ear, then the full grain for the harvest. And those great white giants are full with food enough that *no one* need go hungry. "Therefore do not worry, saying, 'What will we eat?' or 'What will we drink?' or 'What will we wear?' . . . [Y]our heavenly Father knows that you need all these things. But strive first for the kingdom of God and his righteousness, and all these things will be given to you as well" (Matt 6:31–33 NRSV).

Christ the King

Spanish Springs Presbyterian Church, Sparks, Nevada
November 22, 2009

2 Samuel 23:1–7
Revelation 1:4b–8
John 18:33–37

"Where Jesus Reigns"

IN POLITICAL CAMPAIGNS OVER the past thirty years, there has been a lot of debate about what government should and shouldn't do. And in the past few political seasons, there has been a lot of talk about personal faith—candidates trying to out-religion each other, often in ways that seem hard to square with their actual positions on particular issues. But even or especially among those candidates who try to convince us of their superior spirituality, hard political philosophies frequently seem paramount over religious beliefs. Things like toughness on crime and individual rights sometimes trump any specific teaching of the Bible, or end up being couched in imprecise but warm phrases about "American values" or "family values" or "Midwestern values" or some other sort of values whose pedigree, theologically speaking, might be a little fuzzy or even suspect. But we cannot blame the candidates too much—generally speaking, they are only saying what they sense the American people want to hear.

As we ponder the sort of direction our political leaders should take in our towns and counties and states and at the national level, it might be useful to recognize that the Bible offers some rather uncompromising standards about what rulers should and should not do. In the Old Testament, all later kings were judged in comparison to the kingship of David, the greatest ruler of the Jewish nation, the human standard by which every other ruler of Israel throughout history has been measured. Not that David was perfect, either in his personal behavior or in his public administration. He had some tremendous moral failings, and, more than once, the desires of his heart interfered with making clear-headed judgments about national policy. His messy family situations sometimes got in the way of his public responsibilities, rendering scandals of recent years amateurish by comparison. God had warned the people about such problems when they were so insistent on having a king, so intent on having an earthly ruler. But they wanted to be like other nations. So, eventually, they got what they begged for. But in no other nation did the ruler of the people have such a conscious sense of *authority from* and *accountability to* the God who created the entire universe. No ruler of Israel could suppose that the authority to govern came from the *people*; no ruler of Israel could claim to have achieved the throne on the basis of personal *merit*. The selection, everybody understood, was *God's* prerogative; the authority to govern was by *God's* choice; and the job description was to rule over people *justly* and in the fear of *God*. The king of Israel would be "like the light of morning, like the sun rising on a cloudless morning, gleaming from the rain on the grassy land" (2 Sam 23:4 NRSV)—always a welcome blessing, nurturing and pure. So David himself testified with his last words.

But when the Bible speaks of the king ruling "justly," ruling with "justice," it is not a matter of strictly interpreting a law or sending lawbreakers off to jail. "Justice," as the Bible speaks of it, has to do with being trustworthy and honoring commitments in a way that maintains relationships, but also with being fair, which, in the Bible, means being merciful. And of course the term "mercy" doesn't come up in many political speeches these days, because mercy is not the sort of quality that wins votes. But mercy *is* what God *expects* from a *leader*, and, as the *prophets* spoke of how governments should behave, *mercy* means giving special attention to the poor and the outcast and the stranger, epitomized in scripture by widows and orphans and foreigners—those least likely to have other champions, those least likely to be listened to, those least likely to be able to defend themselves against the rich and the powerful. How many people ran for office this year on a platform of forgiving debts and being generous toward aliens? We can argue against mercy on the grounds of economics or sociology, but I don't think we can argue against it on the basis of scripture. We can raise objections about practicalities and preferences, but in that case we are arguing with God. Is the tradition of the *marketplace* our standard of behavior, or is it the command of God? Is our faith in some *economic theory*, or is it in God? Is our goal to serve our *self-interest*, or is it to live according to God's purpose for creation? Is it our *prejudices* that we want our leaders to embody, or our spiritual ideals? Is *our* vision defined by God's faithfulness and mercy, or does our behavior show that we take *our* cues from and give *our* loyalties to some *idol* that is neither faithful nor merciful?

Kingship, in the Bible, is not an historical accident of human achievement. It is the instrument of God to achieve God's purpose of a new creation, living in harmony with each other and with God. The power to govern, the authority to rule, comes rightly from *God*. *Kingship* is a concern for the public well-being—it is a highly communal concept, centered on administering public power especially for the sake of the powerless, the afflicted, the marginal. It's not about helping the wealthy get wealthier or helping the powerful get more power. It's not about making it easier to foreclose on the widows or making sure that foreigners toe the line within our boundaries. It's certainly not about expanding economic empires or imposing a set of cultural standards.

Unfortunately, elective and even appointive politics tends to cater to those who already have wealth and power and status, has a way of appealing to selfish motives and drawing on fear. Even many centuries ago, when a governor was appointed by the Roman emperor to a faraway province that was considered a perpetual trouble spot, for instance, it was *not* for the purpose of showing mercy and exercising generosity and making sure that the outcast and the marginal were housed and fed and treated with kindness. Pontius Pilate had one duty, as far as his superiors were concerned—to keep order, to quell disturbances, to prevent anyone from challenging or questioning Rome's decrees. Oh, the Romans of course saw their rule over Palestine as a generous gift of a superior culture and wisdom and experience, and so they rationalized all sorts of harsh means to justify their arrogant goals. "Mercy" was not in their political vocabulary, and *their* notion of justice was defined not by *God* but by the *ruling* class, who had easy access to the courts.

So when the drama of how the Son of God would fare among the powers and prejudices of the world came down to a trial before the Roman governor of Judea, there was really very little question what the outcome would be. *Rome's* definition of justice would prevail. Order would be kept. Selfish interests would be served. The desires of the powerful would win. Jesus would be put to death. But along the way, in the Bible's telling of the story, it would become clear that it was not really *Jesus* who was on trial, but the *world* and its powers—the forces that were presuming to judge the Son of God, the only true king the world has ever had, perfect in wisdom, perfect in mercy, perfect in ministering to the well-being of humankind, rich and poor, mighty and modest, member of the house of Israel or ritually unclean.

"Are you the king of the Jews?" (John 18:33b NRSV), Pilate asked, either mockingly, or incredulously, or in ignorance. "My kingdom is not from *this* world" (18:36a NRSV), Jesus said. For the world defines kingship in terms of armies and palaces and decrees—weapons and treasures and orders. *That* was the authority that had placed Pilate in the governor's chair. *That* was the authority that concluded that the destiny of the Son of God was the gallows. *That* was the authority that was so afraid of a man who healed the sick and the blind and the lame and fed the hungry and embraced the children and mercifully told those who were grieved by their sins that they were forgiven, free once again to receive and rejoice in the love of God. And not only was *Rome* afraid, but also the leaders of the Jews themselves, who had made a nice career of telling their people that they must wait, always wait, for some *future* day of justice and mercy. Imagine what would happen if people started living like Jesus was really king! Think of the economy, erected on debt and the idolatry of things! Think of foreign relations, founded on the balance of fear and suspicion! Think of the social order, where stability is a matter of everyone knowing their place and staying there! Yes, the emperor and his lieutenant had every reason to shake in their sandals. And so does every king and president and prime minister and governor today who does not lay him- or herself and his or her office at the feet of Jesus Christ and pray that God will make them faithful instruments of the divine will of justice and mercy, every king and president and prime minister and governor today who does not rule in the fear of God.

"Are you the king of the Jews?" (18:33b NRSV), Pilate asked. "My kingdom is not from this world," Jesus said. "My kingdom is not from here" (18:36a, c NRSV). Where, then, *does* Jesus reign? Just exactly who *are* his subjects? He is not *exclusively* concerned with *any* nationality; no government can claim him. That is why it is so problematic to put any national flag in a Christian church. He acted always for the benefit and welfare of those whom society disregarded or cast aside, ministering to their *physical* needs as well as forgiving their sins and encouraging them to faith in God, but he had *wealthy* friends and followers as well—he turned no one away, though he spoke frankly of the difficulty that the well-heeled and well-connected would have putting aside all their securities and achievements and trusting only in him. He blessed the lives of young and old and in-between, women as well as men, in a time when being a child or being a woman was otherwise no great blessing, and being fifty or over was no great privilege, either. He ministered to non-Jews, considered by the legalists and by people in general to be *unworthy* of God's interest, without first insisting that they become good Jews. He even ministered to the enemy—to a Roman centurion, commending him for a superior faith and holding him up as an example for those who reckoned themselves God's special people. Yes, Jesus is a king— is *the* king—who surpassed even David in every category by which David himself admitted a king is to be judged. For this Jesus was born, and for this Jesus came into the world, to testify to the truth as God declares it to be true, not only with his words of instruction and command, but also with his deeds of compassion and mercy.

Where *does* Jesus reign? Just exactly who *are* his subjects? Everywhere, and everyone who listens to his voice—everywhere justice is yearned for and justice is done, everywhere mercy is longed for and mercy is given, everywhere the poor and the oppressed and the outcast cry out and the poor and the oppressed and the outcast are heard; everyone who hears Jesus' voice enjoining us to trust God, to forgive each other, to pour ourselves out in love for neighbors of every sort, and then responds to it as the very truth of God. And any earthly ruler who governs by *these* standards will be "like the light of morning, like the sun rising on a cloudless morning, gleaming from the rain on the grassy land" (2 Sam 23:4 NRSV). And it will be clear to everyone that, in *that* fortunate nation, *Jesus* reigns.

Appendix

MANY PASTORS AND OTHERS who are interested in reviving the practice of daily prayer at morning, mid-day, evening, and close of day, as commended in the Presbyterian Church (U.S.A.) *Directory for Worship* and for which resources are provided in the denomination's *Book of Common Worship*, among other places, have become familiar with the Daily Lectionary. The lections have guided the prayers of readers of the *Mission Yearbook* for many decades. Partly for my own discipline in developing the ability to deal homiletically with any passage of scripture, and partly in order to introduce people to the Daily Lectionary, it has been my practice, if given the option, to preach from its scripture passages whenever I have been invited to deliver the sermon at presbytery and other weekday worship services. The following sermon was delivered at the spring 2009 meeting of the Presbytery of Nevada.

Appendix

Presbytery of Nevada (Daily Lectionary)
First Presbyterian Church, Las Vegas, Nevada
March 10, 2009
Jeremiah 2:1–13, 29–32
Romans 1:16–25
John 4:43–54

"Living Water"

A YEAR AGO, AT our spring gathering of presbytery, I found myself here in Las Vegas with an extra day on which I had no meetings. A day without any particular responsibilities is a rarity for me, and I was eager to make the most of it. I had long wanted to see Valley of Fire State Park, but had never had the opportunity, despite the fact that I have been coming to Las Vegas over the course of a lifetime to visit relatives and, more recently, of course, almost annually for presbytery. Although I didn't have equipment for a long hike, I looked forward to taking whatever short walks I could. It ended up being one of the most enjoyable days of my life; I had no idea the geological formations were so extensive, the scenery so varied, the colors so intense. When I told people about it at the meeting, I was surprised to discover that even many Las Vegas residents among us had never been to the park. Well, I hope you'll remedy that this spring.

One of the walks I took was along a quarter-mile trail to Mouse's Tank, a natural basin in the sandstone that, this time of year, is full of collected rainwater. It's named after an Indian who used it as a hiding place in the 1800s. From what I read in the park brochure, I had been expecting an inviting pool of clear, shimmering water that would have refreshed one even just to look at it. But when I arrived at the end of the trail, I discovered instead a stinking, scum-covered depression that I couldn't imagine *anyone* wanting to drink out of. On a hot day in the Nevada desert, it's hard to turn up your nose at *any* source of water, I suppose, but *this* stuff looked awful, smelled awful, and, I am sure, would have tasted awful.

The next morning, before the presbytery meeting started, I drove out the opposite direction to Red Spring, off of West Charleston Boulevard, and took the nature walk around a spring-fed meadow, a surprising oasis that supports a host of wildlife and was already, last March, carpeted with wildflowers. The water gurgled out of a cavity in the hillside and spread out across the grassy expanse, not more than a few gallons per minute, but clear and pure and miraculously life-giving. What a contrast it was to the putrid stench of Mouse's Tank.

About ten years before the first batch of Judah's elite were deported to Babylon, or about twenty years before Jerusalem fell to the Babylonian army, the prophet Jeremiah prophesied to the people of Jerusalem and Judah: "Be appalled, O heavens, at this, be shocked, be utterly desolate, says the Lord, for my people have committed two evils: they have forsaken me, the fountain of living water, and dug out cisterns for themselves, cracked cisterns that can hold no water" (Jer 2:12–13 NRSV). That was the way it was with cisterns in the Near East, holes dug out of the rock to collect the rainwater when it fell—if the rock had any fissures in it at all, the water would eventually drain away before it could all be used, and in that land every drop was important. If it *didn't* drain out, eventually it became like Mouse's Tank—stagnant and polluted.

That's what the people had settled for, metaphorically, in deciding to turn from the true and living God to scurry after the gods of the land—the Baals, the promisors of fertility, that is, the promisors of the rainfall that produces crops, that is, the promisors of wealth and economic security. It is probable that the gods of Canaan continued to be worshiped here and there from the time Joshua led the Israelites into the Promised Land. It is likely that the worship of Yahweh, who had caused the seawater to part and create a way of exodus from Egypt for the descendants of Abraham, had never fully displaced the worship of idols in the land that was supposed to flow with milk and honey. David consolidated worship in Jerusalem. Solomon built the temple. That might have suppressed the temptation to worship stone calves on high places for a while, but the old habits of bowing down to whoever and whatever promised to meet human desires for prosperity, even to the point of cult prostitution and, some scholars suggest, child sacrifice, kept reasserting themselves over the centuries. "What wrong did your ancestors find in me that they went far from me, and went after worthless things, and became worthless themselves?" (2:5 NRSV), the Lord asked the people through the lips of Jeremiah. "I brought you into a plentiful land to eat its fruits and its good things. But when you entered you defiled my land, and made my heritage an abomination. . . . [T]he rulers transgressed against me; the prophets prophesied by Baal, and went after things that do not profit" (2:7–8 NRSV). They turned their backs on the "fountain of living water" (2:13b NRSV)—God, from whom all blessings flow—and settled instead for cisterns, into which what *used* to be God's refreshing rain collects and stands and turns foul, if it doesn't just disappear altogether. The priests of Baal put on quite a show, as in their contest with Elijah, but their method was to play on fears and uncertainties that enslaved again, in bonds of magic and superstition, the people whom God had set free from Egypt. In the land of plenty, the people of the God who had given manna from the sky nevertheless became anxious over consumption. Their desperate fear of insecurity became their driving motive in matters of both body and spirit.

Those of us who commonly preach on Sundays from the lectionary, and our congregations, may not be so familiar with the story of the *second* sign that Jesus did in Cana. Matthew and Luke tell of a Roman centurion who sought out Jesus in Capernaum to cure his servant of a serious illness, and said that if Jesus only spoke the word, the servant would be healed; Matthew and Luke say that Jesus *commended* the faith of this Gentile, which exceeded even the faith of the Jews. But in today's passage from the *daily* lectionary, the Gospel of *John* tells a somewhat different story of a royal official—who, in the border region of Galilee, might well have been a Gentile, too—whose faith in Jesus' ability to heal prompted him to travel a dozen miles or more to seek out Jesus. In *this* story, curiously, Jesus seems to *condemn* the sort of faith that rests on signs and wonders: "Unless you see signs and wonders, you will not believe" (John 4:48 NRSV).

Since the word "you" here is plural, it may be that Jesus wasn't rebuking the *official*, but the *Galileans* who had welcomed Jesus into their territory, because they had seen him perform miracles in Jerusalem at the Passover. A celebrity was in their midst! They were interested in *him* as they might have been curious about a *magician* or a *wizard*, a diversion from the daily routine, someone new to gossip about. Some, no doubt, wanted a cure for their ailments or the ailments of their friends or relatives, and came to *him* as they would have come to a *physician*, ready to pay, perhaps dearly, for relief from their afflictions. Jesus perceived that these people were not far removed from their ancestors, who were ready to barter any arrangement that would get them what they wanted, even so worthy a goal as an end to discomfort or the threat of death, even if it left them penniless and indebted. Their interest in Jesus rested solely in the prospect that he might choose to *comply* with their request, be it sober or whimsical, and his fame as a wonder worker would grow and perhaps draw large crowds to gawk at his *next* trick. The vast majority of the crowd would miss the point of it all. Their interest in this latest superstar would actually blind them to who he really was, and who had sent him, and why.

As a result of that *other* sign Jesus did at Cana—turning water into wine at a wedding feast that was in danger of becoming boring—the disciples began to discern who Jesus was, but the other wedding guests were probably interested in Jesus only because he had enabled them to party on; the whole episode was premature, as far as Jesus was concerned. He had tried to tell his mother so. But the mission of Jesus was not about making people happy, not even about keeping people healthy, certainly not about making people drunk. It was about giving people life in the most profound sense, in the fullest degree. And so when Jesus came again to Cana, where, John reminds us, Jesus had earlier changed the water into wine, he was encountered by a man who went out of his way to find not just *any* miracle healer, but *Jesus*, because his son was not just *sick*, but at the point of *death*. "'Sir, come down before my little boy dies.'" And Jesus responded not simply, "'Go, your son will be *well* again,'" but, "'Go, your son will *live*.' The man believed the word that Jesus spoke to him and started on his way. As he was going down, his slaves met him and told him"—not just that his son was getting *well* again, but—"that he was *alive*. So he asked them the hour when he began to recover, and they said to him, 'Yesterday at one in the afternoon the fever left him.' The father realized that this was the hour when Jesus had said to him, 'Your son will live.' . . . Now this was the *second* sign that Jesus did after coming from Judea to Galilee" (4:49–54 NRSV).

And *in between* those two signs—in between the turning of collected water into something *more* than water, flowing in lavish abundance, and restoring to life the boy who was on the verge of *death*—John carefully positioned *another* story, one familiar to us all, about a woman who daily had to come out in the noontide heat to let down her bucket into a well, rather like a cistern, and draw it up again and carry it, heavy, back home, weary with her task, weary of her circumstances, in need of cleansing and refreshment more than a bucket's worth of liquid could provide, and encountered there at the well the living water that is Jesus Christ the Son of God, "a spring of water gushing up to eternal life" (4:14b NRSV). And the life-giving spring to which he introduced her, no amount of money could buy, nor need do, but was accessible to her free and without charge on the basis of faith.

The Samaritan woman at the well and the Gentile official both addressed Jesus with a word that is customarily translated here as "Sir." The word is *Kyrie*, translated elsewhere in the New Testament as "Lord." John is famous for using terms that have multiple meanings; one person in the story uses the word to mean one thing, another person, usually Jesus, uses the word to mean something else. Could it be that the official came straight to Jesus because he recognized Jesus to be what the woman at the well had only just begun to suspect—the Lord, who not only *cures*, but gives *life*, and not only a span of *years*, but life *eternal*? "Jesus said to [the official], 'Go; your son will live.' The man believed the word that Jesus spoke to him and went on his way" (4:50 NRSV). And when he learned that his son had begun to recover at the very hour Jesus had said to him, "'Your son will live' . . . he himself believed, along with his whole household" (4:53b NRSV).

Why would anyone be satisfied with that which is *less* than the fountain of living water? Why would anyone dig out cisterns instead and content him- or herself with drinking the runoff, the earth's discard, that soon becomes stagnant and polluted, or else disappears through the cracks and fissures of fault and imperfection? God is not like Baal, whose favor needs to be "bought," nor can it be. God is not some loveless, amoral idol whose delivery of rainfall can be *ordered* or whose working of a cure can be *purchased* and whose worthiness of our worship is directly proportionate to the amount of our bank account or the measure of our popularity or the degree of our physical fitness. The people of Judah in Jeremiah's day had forsaken the God who loved them. Centuries later, the people of Jerusalem and even Galilee, if they misperceived who Jesus was, would willingly abandon him whenever the *next* magician or miracle worker came along; and indeed, when he *forgave* the *unpopular* and *fed* the *unimportant* and *healed* the *unholy*, they *did* abandon him, because they had never opened themselves to the eternal life that he offered.

We live in a culture that expects measurable profit from every activity and places highest value on the sensational. With declining attendance and declining giving and declining influence, the church is tempted as never before to cater to the profit seekers and the sensationalists. But that would be to promote the worship of Baal, to invite people to Christ for what he can *do for us* rather than for *who he is*. Miracles by themselves do not lead to faith. It is the discerning glimpse of God, who is at work *within* the miracle, that is the faith-sparking event, and makes of the *miracle* a *sign*. As one commentator has noted, to see God at work in Jesus' act of healing is to recognize the truth of what John declared in his first chapter: "[T]he Word became flesh and lived among us, and we have seen his glory" (1:14a NRSV). It is the difference between seeing in a miracle either a mere spectacle or a potent symbol of God's merciful love. It is the difference between settling for a stale cesspool or seeking out a spring of water gushing up to eternal life, life that the cross could not destroy, life that the tomb could not contain, life that tumbles from bread broken and wine poured out whenever those who have faith in who Jesus *is* gather at this table in his name. And it has profound implications for what we do in worship, what we do in education, what we do in fellowship, what we do in mission in the Presbyterian Church (U.S.A.) and in each of our congregations.

List of Sources Cited

Brooks, David. *The Road to Character*. New York: Random House, 2015.
Fulghum, Robert. *All I Really Need to Know I Learned in Kindergarten*. New York: Villard Books, 1988.
Keizer, Garret. *A Dresser of Sycamore Trees*. Boston: David R. Godine, 2001.
Swift, Jonathan. *Gulliver's Travels*. Chicago: Donohue & Co., n.d.

www.ingramcontent.com/pod-product-compliance
Lightning Source LLC
Chambersburg PA
CBHW050811160426
43192CB00010B/1724